FINANCIAL SERVICES:

# WOMEN AT THE TOP

A WIFS RESEARCH STUDY

Regina,
All My Best
Love,
Juli

# FINANCIAL SERVICES:
# WOMEN AT THE TOP
## A WIFS RESEARCH STUDY

**ARTHEA REED AND DIANE DIXON**

OPEN BOOK
EDITIONS
A Berrett-Koehler Partner

iUniverse®

# FINANCIAL SERVICES: WOMEN AT THE TOP
## A WIFS RESEARCH STUDY

*iUniverse books may be ordered through booksellers or by contacting:*

*iUniverse*
*1663 Liberty Drive*
*Bloomington, IN 47403*
*www.iuniverse.com*
*1-800-Authors (1-800-288-4677)*

*Because of the dynamic nature of the Internet, any web addresses or links contained in this book may have changed since publication and may no longer be valid. The views expressed in this work are solely those of the author and do not necessarily reflect the views of the publisher, and the publisher hereby disclaims any responsibility for them.*

*Any people depicted in stock imagery provided by Thinkstock are models, and such images are being used for illustrative purposes only. Certain stock imagery © Thinkstock.*

*ISBN: 978-1-4917-7061-0 (sc)*
*ISBN: 978-1-4917-7059-7 (hc)*
*ISBN: 978-1-4917-7060-3 (e)*

*Library of Congress Control Number: 2015909477*

*Print information available on the last page.*

*iUniverse rev. date: 7/31/2015*

*For the amazing women in the
financial services industry—
past, present, and future*

# CONTENTS ————————————————

# ACKNOWLEDGMENTS

*Financial Services: Women at the Top* would not exist without the twenty-three amazing women of the financial services industry who gave their precious time to tell their professional and life stories. We thank them for their forthrightness, honesty, caring, optimism, and, most of all, their willingness to help all who read these pages reach even higher levels of success and satisfaction in their chosen careers. They, along with the relatively few women who preceded them in the financial services industry, have built a strong foundation for all the women who follow. Likewise, the commitment of these twenty-three women and others like them helps ensure the continued strength of an industry that relies on human capital for its success.

Special thanks to these amazing women:

Robelynn H. Abadie (CAP®, RFC, LUTCF, CHRS®, CSA, Founder and CEO Abadie Financial Services, LLC)

Delynn Dolan Alexander (CLTC, Wealth Management Advisor, Founder and Chief Business Development Officer, Alexander Financial Services, Northwestern Mutual)

Colleen M. Bowler (CFP®, Lincoln Financial Advisors–Strategic Wealth Partners, Founder)

Lisa Sappenfield Boyer (CFP®, Registered Principal and Investment Adviser Representative, Owner, Boyer and Sappenfield Investment Advisors, Transamerica Financial Advisors)

Betty Harris Custer (CFP®, CRPC®, Founding Managing Partner, Custer Financial Services, Lincoln Financial Advisors)

Karen L. DeRose (CFP®, CRPC®, Managing Partner, DeRose Financial Planning Group, Lincoln Financial Advisors)

Barbara Brazda Dietze (CLU, ChFC, Financial Adviser, Eagle Strategies LLC, Agent, New York Life)

Antonia (Toni) Espey (CASL, Antonia C. Espey Insurance Agency, Inc., State Farm)

Anne Franklin-Peiper (CLU, ChFC, CASL, Wealth Management Advisor, Northwestern Mutual)

Pamela Gilmour (CPA, CFP®, CLU, ChFC, CASL, Financial Planner and Owner, Financial Fitness, Guardian Life Insurance Company of America)

Kathleen Godfrey (Registered Investment Advisor, President, and CEO, Godfrey Financial Associates)

Nicole Holland-Hong (CFP®, CLU, ChFC, CASL, Wealth Management Advisor, Northwestern Mutual)

Monica A. Jones (FIC, Life Insurance and Annuity Specialist, ACSC-AAA Life Insurance Company)

Gail Linn (CFP®, CASL, ChFC, LUTCF, Financial Services Representative, Financial Planner, MetLife Premier Client Group of NYC)

Juli McNeely (LUTCF, CFP®, CLU, Owner and President, McNeely Financial Services, Inc.)

Anne Machesky (Financial Planner, Sagemark Consulting/Lincoln Financial Advisors)

Ellie Mills (CLU, LUTCF, RFC, Ellie Mills Insurance Agency, Inc., State Farm)

Dianna Parker (CFP®, National Resource, Director of Planning, Southern Regional Planning Group, Sagemark Consulting/Lincoln Financial Advisors)

Donna A. Patton (CLU, ChFC, Registered Representative, Financial Advisor, Principal Financial Group)

Melanie L. Shanty (CRPC®, R.S.S. Financial Services, Inc., Lincoln Financial Advisors)

Ginger Weiss (Senior Partner, Creative Financial Group, Registered Representative, MetLife Securities)

Nancy Wolfe-Smith (CLU, FLMI, LUTCF, MBA, Nancy Wolfe-Smith Insurance Agency, Inc., State Farm)

Paula Zonin (CLU, ChFC, LUTCF, Vice President, Brokerage Manager, and Disability Income Specialist, National Financial Network, LLC, General Agency of Guardian Life Insurance Company of America)

Our thanks also go to the companies in the financial services industry who referred these women to us and supported the women's participation in this research project: AAA, Guardian Life Insurance Company, Lincoln Financial Advisors, MetLife, New England Financial Group, New York Life, Northwestern Mutual, Principal Financial Group, State Farm, and Transamerica Financial Advisors.

Without the support, funding, and encouragement of WIFS (Women in Insurance and Financial Services), this research project would never have been started. The *WIFS Survey for Highly Successful Women in the Financial Services Industry*,[1] completed in 2012, was administered and the results compiled by the managerial team of WIFS. Thank you.

Because of the regulatory environment under which the financial services industry operates, complying with all rules and regulations is critical for all publications associated with the industry. Diana Moro-Goane provided us with her independent, expert compliance review and advice. We are very grateful.

*Making More Room for Women in the Financial Planning Profession*,[2] a research study initiated by Nancy Kistner, 2013 chair of the Certified Financial Planner (CFP) Board of Standards, is a groundbreaking research study designed to determine "reasons for the dearth of women Certified Financial Planner® professionals." Because this "inquiry needed to be bold, groundbreaking, and comprehensive in scope," it provides information that applies to female financial planners and all women and companies in the financial services industry. We are grateful to Nancy Kistner and the CFP® Board Standards for allowing us to utilize their research to corroborate the information gleaned from The *WIFS Survey for Highly Successfully Women in the Financial Services Industry* survey and the interviews conducted for this book. We are, indeed, all on the same page!

We are convinced that the combined research and publication of the CFP® and WIFS studies will help more women enter and succeed in the financial services industry. Because we—and others—have documented that women can succeed at the same level as their male counterparts, we trust that this book will encourage women to enter the industry, persist and survive the early difficult years, and achieve success in their own unique ways. We also believe this book and other similar publications will help educate financial services industry leaders in the great potential of women to succeed and improve the advice, products, and services provided by the industry to clients and consumers. Likewise, the advice of the twenty-three amazingly successful women in this book and the research studies that support its authenticity can help those who recruit and train women (and men) provide a supportive environment and appropriate policies and procedures to help ensure their success.

Most importantly, this book can help all who enter the industry thrive within it and say, "I love what I do."

We are incredibly appreciative of the small role we have been able to play in helping women achieve the success they deserve and making this amazing industry a better place for all who work in it and benefit from it. We trust that the women (and men) who read this book will pass it on to others who can utilize this research and advice to grow their own careers and improve the service they provide to their clients.

The financial services industry has given us both successful and worthwhile careers. We have been able to pass this wealth on to our clients and others we have touched. We are both incredibly appreciative of all who have helped make this possible.

—Arthea (Charlie) Reed and Diane Dixon

# INTRODUCTION ────────────────────────

## ARTHEA (CHARLIE) REED, PHD, CLTC

In 1996, I changed careers from being a professor and chairperson of the University of North Carolina–Asheville Department of Education to being a financial representative with Northwestern Mutual. Many of my professorial colleagues thought the career shift was unthinkable. "There is no better job than being a full professor," many told me. And, on the one hand, I had to agree. I loved teaching, had already authored or coauthored at least ten books, had been the editor of an international journal in the field of adolescent literature, and had been selected by my colleagues as the Feldman Professor of Research and Service. I had traveled nationally and internationally, teaching, doing research, and providing international experiences for my students. It was a great job. Was I crazy?

No, I decided, I was not crazy. I had bumped my head against academia's glass ceiling that keeps many women professors from earning as much as their male colleagues. My boss, the vice chancellor for academic affairs, said, "Charlie, I can't give you any more raises until I bring other female faculty up to your salary." I asked if there were any male faculty with similar experience and salaries higher than mine. Of course, I knew his answer was yes. However, it was his job to reward faculty with merit pay, treat faculty *equitably* (his word), and keep the peace.

So I began to consider my options. Financial services made sense on several fronts:

1. The only glass ceiling in the entrepreneurial financial services industry is the one we place above our own heads.
2. I would still be teaching, but now I would be teaching clients to make good decisions about their finances.
3. In the entrepreneurial world of financial services, particularly after the difficult early years, there is a great deal of scheduling flexibility. So I wouldn't have to give up research, writing, or traveling.
4. I could do the job in my hometown and didn't have to uproot my family to move to a university somewhere across the state or country.
5. My husband had been in the financial services industry for two decades and would become my manager and mentor.

So I made the move and never looked back. This is not to say it was easy, but I did have the advantage of a manager who knew and respected my needs and abilities and was committed to helping me become a success. He also had his own team of professionals and staff who could assist me in my business while assisting him in his.

## DIANE DIXON, CLU

Not long after I started my new career, I met Diane Dixon, who was then Assistant Director–Recruitment. The first time I saw Diane was at an event she sponsored for all Northwestern Mutual women following an annual Sunday morning 5K walk or run at the company's major meeting in July. Run to Success was part networking, part education, part inspiration, and part pep rally for an enthusiastic group of women, many of whom were financial representatives. The room was packed, the panel was inspirational, and the entire event made me very glad about my decision to change careers.

However, at the same event the following year, I realized that all of the women with whom I had networked at Run to Success the prior year were no longer with the company, and most were no longer in the industry. What had happened? Why had these bright, enthusiastic women left such a promising career before they knew what the career had to offer? Diane and her team were also asking those questions and many more about why women were not joining the industry and remaining in it at the same rate as men.

By the time I attended the second Run to Success, Diane and I had had numerous conversations about the career and how best to succeed in it. Diane was a great mentor. Unlike me, she had joined Northwestern Mutual during her freshman year of college, and 2015 marked her thirty-eighth year working in the financial services industry. Her first job was as the assistant to a very supportive district agent. She later became a successful financial representative. After twelve years building a successful practice, Diane was tapped by Northwestern Mutual to spearhead the corporate initiative focused on women as financial representatives. She was a very good choice.

Many of her colleagues thought her decision to leave her successful practice and head to the corporate world was unthinkable. Her decision to make the career change was largely driven by her desire to

- create awareness of career opportunities for women in the financial services industry;
- encourage and challenge corporate and agency leadership to extend their recruiting efforts to a *new talent pool* and adjust their corporate and office environments to make the career more welcoming and productive for women; and
- support and encourage women already in the industry as she had been supported over the years.

Diane left Northwestern Mutual in 2000 and launched her own professional coaching practice. Shortly thereafter, she became my business coach. I frequently tell Diane that my decision to hire her to work with my team and me was the best business decision I ever made. Today, Diane helps many female and male financial services professionals and their teams from across the industry build successful practices.

While Diane was my coach, she became president of WIFS (Women in Insurance and Financial Services), the only national professional organization focused on the needs of women in the financial services industry. Diane was named WIFS Woman of the Year in 2008 because of her extensive work and commitment to helping advance the careers of women in the financial services industry. Diane encouraged me to join WIFS and become involved. I did, and in 2009, I was selected to serve on the WIFS board of directors.

Both Diane and I were fortunate to be mentored by men in leadership who supported and respected us as individuals and did not try to make us fit into a professional world with procedures and goals largely developed by men to assist men in becoming successful in the career. They also did not lower their expectations of us, and they never hesitated to challenge us to succeed. They connected us to others in our company and the industry, helping us become engaged and included. And they enjoyed cheering us on to success. Were our environments perfect? No. However, even though imperfect, we were able to grow and succeed in those environments due to the support of effective leaders and mentors. We wish the same for women who are now in the industry and those who will join it in the future.

We believe this book will help the women and men who read it become the successful professionals their clients and the industry need. Further, we hope and believe the WIFS research study and this capstone book will be the primers that help turn the financial services industry into one that excels in attracting, developing, and fully embracing female financial services professionals. Doing so will make the industry more attractive and stronger for all.

## THE WIFS RESEARCH STUDY

The mission of WIFS,[3] a national professional organization founded in 1936 by six successful women who met at a Million Dollar Round Table (MDRT)[4] meeting, is to *attract, develop, and advance* women in the financial services industry. But, in spite of the long history of WIFS and the good work they do on behalf of women, the question still remains: Why are there are so few women professionals in the financial services industry? In 2011, the board of directors of WIFS authorized a multiyear research study in an attempt to determine what attracts women to the industry, what makes them successful throughout their careers, and what keeps them growing and achieving. The research began with an industry-wide survey and culminates with this book. More information about this research project will be discussed in the next section on "Research Methodology."

Although it is difficult to determine the exact number of women in the industry, most studies, including the self-reporting of large corporations, place women financial professionals at less than 20 percent of the total. This seems counterintuitive to women who have succeeded in the industry. Financial services is a people-centered career in which financial professionals help individuals, families, and businesses achieve financial independence. The career offers great flexibility to women who frequently must juggle the needs of their children and the demands of their jobs. And the more financially successful her clients become, the more financially successful she will be.

What are the goals of the WIFS research and this book?

1. To inspire financial services preprofessionals and professionals at all levels
2. To understand what successful female financial services professionals have done to achieve their success
3. To educate new and experienced female financial services professionals and the leaders who train them on how these successful practices can be replicated
4. To increase awareness of what makes financial services workplaces inclusive, inspirational, and encouraging for all
5. To provide role models and examples for others who can benefit from the stories of the amazingly successful women featured in this book

An important goal of this book is to provide you (future and current financial professionals) with inspirational information about what makes the most successful women in the financial services industry tick. You will learn what these women have done to achieve their success. You will hear how they have overcome great personal tragedy, professional ridicule, and failure. And, the roadmap at the end of the book will help you understand how you can do the same whether you are already in the industry or are considering it for your career.

The book is written to help the reader determine what successful women in the financial services industry believe about the work they do and what they have done to achieve their success. Throughout this book, you will read stories about the professional and personal journeys of many of the most financially successful women in the industry. Although all of the women featured in the book have achieved financial success at the level of their most successful male peers, they do not talk about their success in terms of what they earn or the company recognition they have received. Rather, they talk about their success in terms of the business and personal goals they have set and met and how they have helped their clients achieve their financial goals. They discuss how they encourage their team members and colleagues to reach higher than they dreamed imaginable, how important their children are to them—and how they play an active role in their lives—and the commitment they make to paying it forward and giving back.

This does not mean that these women do not recognize the importance of their earnings to their families, lives, careers, clients, and philanthropy. They are realists, and they know that without their significant earnings, their children would not have the opportunities that their wealth has afforded them. They also recognize that they would not be able to assist their parents and other adult family members in times of medical and financial crisis. Nor would they be able to give back to their communities and the profession at the levels they do. Similarly, it is the success they have achieved in the companies they represent that has given them the unique opportunity available to only the biggest producers for advanced learning, sophisticated technology, high-powered advisors, and specialized products that allow them to serve their clients at the highest levels. What seems to make these women unique, however, is that they are not motivated by money, and they do not consider what they earn or industry or company recognition amongst their most important achievements.

Another goal of the WIFS research study and book is to convert the workplaces of all female and male financial professionals into centers of inspiration, growth, and professionalism. This goal requires the commitment of corporate and field management as well as educational institutions and professional organizations that provide the education and training to financial professionals. Reading this book, learning what these successful women tell us about who helped them along the way and what they did to become successful, and using this information to design and implement plans and procedures that encourage the professional growth of women and men can change the workplace to one of inclusion, growth, and stability.

Our hope is that all who purchase this book will buy two copies: one for herself or himself and one for someone else. Giving the book to someone else (a person new to the business, a colleague, a manager, a family member, a friend, or the child of a friend) is a way to pay forward what this great industry has given to you. If you are not in the financial services industry, giving the book is a means of sharing a career option and a path to success that can lead to great professional satisfaction and the opportunity to help hundreds (maybe even thousands) of clients become financially secure and independent.

Who can benefit from reading this book? This book is written for

- women and men considering a career in financial services;
- those in the first few years of a career in financial services;
- financial services professionals with successful practices who want to grow them to a new level but are not quite sure how to do so;
- financial professionals who are experiencing stagnation of their businesses or those who just need a few good ideas to move their business forward;
- women and men who have successful practices and want to grow them to new levels or in new directions;
- women and men planning to transition their practices to the next generation of financial professionals;
- corporate and field management; and

- colleges, universities, corporations, and managers who provide education and training for financial services preprofessionals and professionals.

If you are considering a career in financial services, whether you are just completing your education or have worked in another profession for many years, the stories of the women featured in this book can help you determine if the career is a good fit for you. For those who have recently started a financial services career, the journeys these women have taken will help you determine what steps you need to take to begin your own journey.

This book is not only for women. Men who read the book can also benefit from the success stories related by these women. As men assume more responsibility for their children, the tales of how these women have not simply juggled or balanced motherhood and career, but blended their families and their practices can provide encouragement for how they can do the same.

If you have been in the financial services industry for a number of years and your practice has stopped growing or you are tired and bored, you can benefit from this book. Not all the women featured in this book were immediate stars. Some of them had relatively slow starts or even changed jobs and started from scratch later. However, they persevered and became tremendously successful. Many of the steps they took could help you revitalize your practice.

Perhaps you are simply seeking a few good ideas to move your business to the next level. This book is also for you. The journeys these women have taken will give you lots of ideas that spark new growth in your practice.

If you are a financial services professional who is planning to transition your practice to the next generation, you can learn from the experiences of many of these successful women. For them, a succession plan, while important, is not enough. What they seek is sustaining their practices beyond their full-time involvement in them. They are not looking for someone to merely transfer their client files to; instead, they are seeking ways to maintain their business and sustain the level of service their clients have come to expect into the next generation. How they are doing this, the problems that have occurred, and some surprises along the way can provide the inspiration and techniques you need to do the same.

Field and corporate management can also benefit from reading this book. The steps these women have taken to reach the pinnacle of success can be replicated. It takes more than developing curricula, organizing meetings, and providing administrative support services to be a supportive manager. Managers must ask about and understand the needs of their female and male financial service professionals and help them develop career paths in which career and family are blended into workplaces that are aesthetically pleasing, welcoming, private, and safe. Information about what has made the nearly one thousand women who participated in various levels of the WIFS research study successful will allow the managers to build agencies, offices, and companies with climates, policies, and procedures that encourage the career growth of female as well as male financial professionals. If this occurs, the authors of this study are convinced that many more women and men will enter the industry and remain in the industry for their professional lifetimes.

The stories of these incredibly successful women can also assist those corporations and educational institutions that train current and future financial professionals to tailor their training to the needs of women as well as men. Most women seek knowledge before they act. If educational institutions can provide training, some leading to professional designations, such as the CFP® (Certified Financial Planner), to students prior to completion of their degree programs, they will enter their new profession armed with the knowledge they need to get started in the business quickly. This will result in earlier success, keeping more women and men in the business.

The book could also be a good textbook or supplemental reading book for students in college or university business, insurance, finance, or sales programs at the undergraduate or graduate level. This research-based book provides ideas, advice, and other information that is reliable and can be replicated.

## HOW TO READ THIS BOOK

The first eight chapters can simply be read and enjoyed. These chapters focus on the amazingly successful women selected and interviewed for this book. The first time each woman is identified, you will also see her current professional title, her professional credentials, and the name of her company and any other company she represents. For a complete list of this information, consult the acknowledgments at the front of the book.

The financial services profession, like most professions, is an alphabet soup of acronyms. In this book, you will find many acronyms designating the names of professional organizations and professional designations. To help you keep them straight and learn more about them, you will find two tables in appendix D at the back of the book. One has the acronyms, names, and websites of professional organizations. The other contains the same information for professional designations.

Chapter 9 is a roadmap for anyone who is considering a career in the financial services industry, is beginning that career, or has been in the industry for five or more years. It can help you determine your next and best steps prior to and throughout your career in the financial services industry. The advice in chapter 9 comes from the nearly eight hundred women who responded to the 2012 WIFS Survey and the twenty-three amazing women interviewed for this book. The chapter concludes with a checklist to help you keep track of how well you are doing on your own personal, professional journey along the road to success.

Chapter 10 summarizes the contributions of the twenty-three women featured in this book to their families, clients, communities, and the financial services profession. The chapter concludes with a narrative about what each of the audiences for whom this book was written can take away from it to make their careers, the careers of future generations, and the financial services industry even better than it is today.

In the appendixes, you will find

A. the 2012 WIFS Survey instrument—without responses;
B. a 2012 article, "Women in Financial Services: How to Succeed in Business," from *GAMA International Journal*[5] (The article,

written by Arthea Reed and Karen Roberts, summarizes many of the finding of the "*WIFS Survey for Highly Successfully Women in the Financial Services Industry.*");

C. the initial interview questions for the women selected and interviewed for this book; and

D. professional organizations and designations: acronyms, descriptions, and websites.

$$\approx$$

To say that interviewing these women, listening to their stories, and sharing them with you has been a privilege is an understatement. Every one of these amazing and real women has made us proud to be women in this wonderful industry. We wish for you the opportunity to say—after many years of serving your clients—as all of these women and we have said, "I love what I do!"

# RESEARCH METHODOLOGY ————————

This book, *Financial Services: Women at the Top—A WIFS Research Study*, is the culmination of a major, multiyear research project initiated in 2011 by the professional organization Women in Insurance and Financial Services (WIFS). In this summary of the research, you will find a description of goals, procedures, characteristics of participants, and intended audiences of each component of the research study.

The overall goal is to determine what makes women successful in the financial services industry.

The procedures used to reach this goal are outlined below.

## WIFS SURVEY FOR HIGHLY SUCCESSFUL WOMEN IN THE FINANCIAL SERVICES INDUSTRY

1.  The *WIFS Survey for Highly Successful Women in the Financial Services Industry*:[6]
    *   Goal of the Survey: Retrace the career paths of the most financially successful women in the industry and determine how taking those routes bring them such achievement.
    *   The questions were designed on a Likert scale, using Constant Contact software. Anecdotal comments were also encouraged. The questions were field tested by having members of the WIFS board complete the survey instrument prior to its distribution. (See appendix A for survey questions.)
    *   The survey was distributed to women financial services professionals via the WIFS website. E-mail announcements and

a link to the online survey were sent to female financial professionals of WIFS corporate partners by their home office personnel. The following were WIFS corporate partners at the time of the survey: Guardian Life Insurance Company of America, Lincoln Financial Group, MassMutual Financial Group, New York Life Insurance Company, Northwestern Mutual Life Insurance Company, the Penn Mutual Life Insurance Company, the Prudential Insurance Company of America, Thrivent Financial for Lutherans, and Transamerica Agency Network. Also the survey was *spidered* (sent to known very successful women, asking them to send the link to the survey to other successful women). The spidering was done by members of the WIFS board and female leadership of other financial services organizations. In addition, sessions at the WIFS 2011 annual conference encouraged attendees and corporate partners to participate in the survey. (There is no way to estimate the number of women invited to participate in the study, but it certainly reached several thousand.)

- The survey closed in April 2012.
- Results were compiled and analyzed based on the self-reported annual gross income of the 794 female financial services professionals who completed the survey.
- The following income levels were used to analyze the data:
  - <$75,000
  - $75,000–$124,999
  - $125,000–$199,999
  - $200,000–$499,999
  - $500,000–$999,999
  - >$1,000,000

  (Note: More than 50 percent of the respondents reported an annual gross income of greater than $200,000.)
- The data was analyzed based on differences in how women at various income levels responded to the questions.

2. An article reporting the outcomes of the survey, "Women in Financial Services: How to Succeed in Business"[7] by Arthea

Reed and Karen Roberts, appeared in *GAMA International Journal*, November/December 2012. (See appendix B for a copy of the article.)

3. Sessions related to survey outcomes were conducted at the professional conferences of GAMA (General Agents Management Association), MDRT (Million Dollar Round Table), NAIFA (National Association of Insurance and Financial Advisors), and WIFS in 2012 and 2013.

4. Although the results of the survey provided some interesting information about the education, training, habits, lifestyles, goals, and business models of the most financially successful female representatives, it also left many questions unanswered.

This book focuses on a select group of highly successful female financial services professionals.

## 1. FINANCIAL SERVICES: WOMEN AT THE TOP

In October 2013 the board of WIFS agreed to have Arthea Reed, author of the survey, and Diane Dixon, business coach, write a book focusing on twenty or more of the most successful female financial services professionals.

The intended audiences of the book were to include

➤ current and future professionals in the financial services industry, particularly—but not only—women;

➤ managers and trainers of professionals in the financial services industry;

➤ leadership of companies and associations in the financial services industry who recruit and train women; and

➤ colleges and universities that provide academic programs in business, financial services, and other related fields.

The goals of the book, as described to the women invited to participate in the study, are as follows:

- reliable research study of successful women in the financial services industry
- broad-based survey of women in the industry
- interviews of large numbers of women earning more than $250,000 per annum in the financial services industry
- readable and accessible
- provide information for leaders, managers, educators, professionals, and future professionals about how to be successful in the career
- help attract more women to the profession and promote women's achievement within the profession
- provide a study of successful women in the career to rival the study done by O. Alfred Granum of successful men in the insurance industry ("Building a Financial Services Clientele: The Ultimate Guide to the One Card System,"[8] eleven editions since 1968)
- provide a roadmap to women about what they can do to achieve maximum success in the career

The women to be featured in the book were identified as follows:

- Each of the corporate partners of WIFS were asked to identify female field representatives who earn at least $250,000 per annum and who were likely to be willing to provide information about their careers and lives that could help other women succeed in the business. Each of these women was sent an e-mail telling her of her nomination and asking her to participate in the interview process for the book.
- Women who completed the 2012 WIFS survey and earned more than $200,000 per year were sent an e-mail and invited to participate in the interview process for the book.
- Women who qualified for the WIFS Circle of Excellence, earning more than $250,000 per year, were sent an e-mail and invited to participate in the interview process.
- Women leaders of professional organizations in the industry were sent an e-mail and invited to participate in the interview process.

More than 140 women were invited to participate in the interview process for the book.

> ➤ Forty-three of these women agreed to participate in the first round of interview questions, which were designed to provide demographic information (i.e., age she entered the business, current age, married or life partner, children and current ages) that were not easily accessible in the survey data analysis.
> ➤ Twenty-three of these forty-three women agreed to participate in a much longer interview process, which required them to complete in writing the answers to nine detailed questions with numerous parts. (See appendix C for a list of the initial questions to which all twenty-three women responded.)
> ➤ All twenty-three women participated in further interviews to provide additional information or answer clarifying questions.
> ➤ The twenty-three women selected and agreeing to participate in the long interview process represent a diverse population of successful female financial services professionals. Their business models and the companies for whom or the broker-dealers with whom they work vary greatly.

Characteristics of the women featured in this book:

✓ ethnically and racially diverse
✓ independent, affiliated with no specific company
✓ captive agents of a single company
✓ wealth managers or financial planners who work with a variety of broker-dealers
✓ financial representatives of large mutual or stock companies
✓ DBA (doing business as) identities
✓ managers and producers for large corporations; may also own their own practices
✓ business owners, with or without partners
✓ sole practitioners with teams of employees

✓ agents for companies whose primary business is neither insurance nor investments
✓ a combination of two or more of the above

Most of the women are currently married with children. Some of the currently married women were single mothers during the early years of growing their businesses. They conduct their businesses in urban centers, small towns, and rural areas.

Each of the twenty-three successful female financial services professionals defines success in a unique way. What she earns is not a part of this definition:

- Each of these women is financially successful.
  - Most earn more than $500,000 annually.
  - Four earn more than $1,000,000 annually.
  - At least two of these women have earned more than $10,000,000 in a single year.

# CHAPTER 1

# SUCCESS STORIES

> Long ago, when I wanted to be the first female agent of the year for Lincoln, my husband advised me that to do so I would have to change. I'd have to stop much of the community service and do less with our children's activities. I determined then, and have never regretted, that this was too high a price to pay. So I have been content with being in the top fifty of five thousand planners most years, but never number one.
>
> Betty Harris Custer, CFP®, CRPC®, Founding Managing Partner, Custer Financial Services, Lincoln Financial Advisors

Women in the financial services industry measure success internally. *Success.* What is it? How do I know when I have reached it? How do I measure it? Is it the same for everyone?

In 2012, 794 female financial services professionals completed a survey, conducted by Women in Insurance and Financial Services (WIFS).[9] In this survey and subsequent interviews with some of the most successful women in the industry, as measured by income, industry-wide recognition, and company recommendations, we have begun to focus on a clear picture of how these women measure success and how they have achieved it.

The women who completed the 2012 survey had many different definitions of success. However, the most highly compensated women (50 percent of survey respondents with annual gross incomes between

1

$200,000 and more than $1,000,000) were less likely to be motivated by extrinsic rewards such as income or recognition. Instead, the intrinsic, internal motivators of achieving their own goals and helping others succeed were significantly more important to them than income or recognition from their companies and the industry.

Does this mean that highly compensated female financial professionals are not interested in what they earn or the recognition they receive? No. These high-achieving women, successful by every measure, consider their income to be important because it provides them with the financial and personal independence and flexibility to live their lives as they choose.

Betty Harris Custer and her husband, Corkey, celebrate her success in business and philanthropy.

## FINANCIAL SUCCESS TRANSLATES INTO MEMBERSHIP IN CORPORATE AND ENTREPRENEURIAL LEADERSHIP GROUPS

The recognition they receive from their companies and the industry, based most often on what they earn and the amount of business they do, is also important. However, it is *not* for the recognition itself. Recognition from their companies and from the industry provides admission to peer groups of the most successful financial services professionals of both genders. As members, these women can participate in think tanks and study groups with the most intelligent and creative minds in the industry. Being a part of such a peer group may also provide these women with additional services and privileges from their companies. What they learn from their peers and the additional assistance they get from the best and brightest in their companies and throughout the industry provides them with knowledge, skills, and ideas that directly benefit their businesses and the sophisticated work they do with their clients. And at the end of the day, this is what these highly successful women say is most important to them.

Angela Shay (left), 2014 President of WIFS, presenting the WIFS Woman of the Year Award to Nancy Wolfe-Smith.

Nicole Holland-Hong (CFP®, CLU, ChFC, CASL, Wealth Management Advisor, Northwestern Mutual) tells financial representatives in her company, "Whether it's your first or fifteenth year, you can make Forum (the Northwestern leaders' group) a goal."

Barbara Brazda Dietze (CLU, ChFC, Financial Adviser, Eagle Strategies LLC, Agent, New York Life) explains why setting a goal for yourself is incredibly important to your success. Barbara learned early in her career while analyzing Earl Nightingale's tape *The Strangest Secret*[10] with a study group of young agents in her agency that "you become what you think about." If what you think about is achieving the goal of membership in the leaders' group of your company, you will do it, no matter the barriers in front of you. Nicole achieved this important benchmark at age forty while she was pregnant with her first child. In the same year, she took a two-month leave of absence after the birth of her son.

One highly compensated female financial services professional in the 2012 survey said, "Doing what I love with those I love—earning a good income and being able to travel and meet some of the most successful people in America (my clientele) ... It doesn't get any better."

Over and over again in the survey and interviews, very successful female financial services professionals talked about their *passion for helping others.* "Most days I feel as though I am helping my friends (clients) achieve financial security and freedom. So it never feels like work." For these women, the most important measure of their success is *loving what they do and for whom they do it* and, as one woman said, "having my clients say: 'My life is better for having known you.'"

Nicole Holland-Hong and her young son enjoy some time together.

# THE SUCCESS STORIES OF FOUR AMAZING WOMEN IN THE FINANCIAL SERVICES INDUSTRY

In this chapter, we will highlight the success stories of four highly compensated, caring female financial services professionals. Of the twenty-three women who were selected and agreed to participate in in-depth interviews for this book, we chose four to help illustrate how different career paths, geographic locations, types of companies and services provided, and personal life stories can all lead to success within the wonderful, diverse world of financial services. The stories of the nineteen other women, all of whom are equally compelling, will be featured throughout the subsequent chapters of this book.

## ARE YOU MAKING A DIFFERENCE IN THE LIVES OF OTHERS?

Robelynn H. Abadie (CAP®, RFC, LUTCF; CHRS®, CSA, Founder and CEO Abadie Financial Services, LLC) reports that she has been "like a sponge" throughout her incredibly successful career in Baton Rouge, Louisiana. She has never stopped learning or seeking mentors. Today, Robelynn is the sole proprietor of her own company (Abadie Financial Services, LLC) with a support staff of three. Robelynn's company is "highly concentrated in corporate/employee benefits." She works primarily with companies with one hundred or more high-net-worth employees (largest group has 1,200 employees). For these companies and employers, her company does "all retirement planning (401k, etc.), health, dental, life, and disability coverage (both group and individual through payroll); key man, buy-sell arrangement; ERISA support; ancillary benefits (critical care, cancer, accidental, etc.)."

She plans to sell the benefits portion of her business within the next three to five years so that she can concentrate on the other, more fulfilling component of her business: life insurance for individuals and business owners, charitable gifts of life insurance, individual disability, annuities, variable products, and mutual funds. Robelynn reports that she has "a lot of personal involvement in the charitable space." She serves on numerous boards and volunteers for many charities. "My hope is that, through the use of planning tools and life insurance, I can assist charities in their fund-development programs." She has recently completed a CAP (Chartered Advisor in Philanthropy) designation from the American College to distinguish herself in this field. While she was working on this designation, she was a part of a study group of twelve men and women who met every other week. In addition to herself, the group included two other insurance professionals, three financial planners, a CPA, and five nonprofit leaders. "It was a lofty crew representing most of the largest charities in the area." Although she has been in the business for more than thirty-six years, she has never stopped learning or providing more knowledgeable information and service to her clients. She is not afraid to allow her business to evolve as her life introduces her to new passions.

Robelynn Abadie, past-president of the MDRT (Million Dollar Round Table) Foundation, appears on the main stage at the MDRT annual meeting.

Robelynn's early years in the business were lonely and difficult (this will be explored in more depth in chapter 2), but through continuously seeking new mentors, coaches, professional designations, and her commitment to volunteerism, she has grown her business to the highest levels. For the past five years, she has qualified for the Million Dollar Round Table's "Top of the Table," a recognition given to the top 2 percent of insurance professionals worldwide. Membership in MDRT is only available to insurance and financial services professionals who earn at least $156,000 (2014) per year from financial services products. TOT membership requires earning at least $936,000 (2014) annually. Although we will not address juggling career and family until later in the book (chapter 4), it is important to note that Robelynn, with the assistance of her husband Wayne, has achieved all of this while nurturing five children.

Here is how Robelynn evaluates her own success and the advice she gives to other women in the financial services industry:

> You can work hard, study, be a mom, a wife, a significant other, a woman who wields much power and influence, but at the end of the day, the key to it all is … are you happy, are you loved and are you making a difference in the life of others?

## BEING A WOMAN IS NOT A DISADVANTAGE; IT IS A PRIVILEGE.

Monica A. Jones (FIC, Life Insurance and Annuity Specialist, ACSC-AAA Life Insurance Company) is unusual among the financial services industry's highly compensated women. She came to financial services rather late in her career and has only been in the industry for nine years. A decade ago she would have never expected to be a life insurance and annuities specialist for ACSC-AAA Life in Chula Vista, California.

Monica had been teaching high school for eighteen years; she loved her job and planned to continue to teach indefinitely. But all of that changed in 2000 when her husband of twenty years suffered a fatal heart attack at age fifty-two. He died without life insurance. He had been a business consultant who charged his clients a part of his fee upfront and the rest when the work was completed. When he died unexpectedly, his clients who had paid the initial fee wanted money refunded for work that had not been done—money the family had already spent. Suddenly Monica was a young widow with a thirteen-year-old daughter, only her teacher's salary, and lots of bills and debts. Her teaching salary could not meet all the unplanned expenses and provide the day-by-day and long-term support for her daughter and herself. And teaching did not have the scheduling flexibility she needed to care for her daughter as a single parent. Leaving a classroom full of high school students to pick up her sick daughter at school simply would not work. She had to find another career.

Her newfound passion for the importance of life insurance, as well as the high-income potential and flexible schedule of a career in insurance made it the ideal choice for her. She joined ACSC-AAA Life Insurance Company, and with the help of her manager and mentor who taught her the products and how to succeed in the business, she quickly rose to the top. Monica writes approximately 200 life insurance policies each year and has more than fifteen-hundred clients. She has qualified for Million Dollar Round Table (MDRT) for nine years. She was ACSC-AAA Life "Rookie of the Year" in her first year in the business. She continues to earn top honors in her company, placing in the top four producers in the Auto Club Enterprises (ACE) from 2006 to 2014 and in the top five producers nationwide every year since she started in the business. In 2009, she was the first female life insurance and annuity specialist named ACSC-AAA Life "Life Agent of the Year" and top producer in the nation; she accomplished this again in 2013.

Monica Jones is honored as the 2013 ACSC-AAA Life "Life Agent of the Year."

Monica, named Woman of the Year in 2012 by WIFS, attributes her success to her work ethic, organizational skills, attitude, and morals. She is an excellent teacher who is able to simply explain the complexities of life insurance and annuities. Monica surrounds herself with successful people. By doing so, she quickly becomes a part of their group and learns from them. She is active in her company, in professional organizations, and in her community. Lifelong learning and constantly improving what she does is part of her being. She believes that through hard work, both she and her clients are rewarded. She has been so successful that her company made a video about how she conducts her business. *A Day in Monica's Life* is presented to every new ACSC-AAA agent during her or his initial training.

Monica believes that her woman's personal touch makes her a better insurance agent and more appreciated by her clients. Each of her clients has his or her own customized plan. After she develops the plan with her clients, Monica stays in touch with them, not using social media or technology, but by sending handwritten personal notes to each of them about four times a year. She admits that this is a big task with more than one thousand clients, but it is well worth it. Her clients do not forget her; they return to do more business with her. They also feed her new business by referring new clients without her even asking. They call her to thank her for her thoughtfulness. She does all of this as the only life insurance professional in her office and with no assistant.[11]

Most importantly, Monica believes in doing what is right for her clients. She is a good listener and does a lot of fact-finding, asking each client difficult questions. And she is committed to the importance of owning life insurance, no matter a client's age. "The best part of this business," says Monica, "is that at the end of the day, you protected another man, woman, child, or family, and you go to sleep knowing their financial future will be secure."

## THINGS MY MOTHER TAUGHT ME

Delynn Dolan Alexander (CLTC, Wealth Management Advisor, Founder and Chief Business Development Officer, Alexander Financial Services, Northwestern Mutual) is a second-generation Northwestern Mutual financial representative. Her mother Elaine Dolan was a single mom and an insurance agent in Dallas when there were almost no women at either company or professional organization meetings. Today, the number of female financial services professionals is still small, less than 20 percent of the industry. However, when Elaine was an active agent, there were no lines at the women's restroom, and some places didn't even have a restroom for women. In spite of the lack of female role models, Elaine was a successful agent and a very successful mom. Delynn knew she wanted to follow in her mom's footsteps by the time she was twelve.

> My mother raised me as a single parent who found herself in the insurance business after meeting with a financial representative to purchase some for herself. She had a work ethic like no one I've ever seen before or after, and she was determined this career would make a difference in our lives by making a difference in her clients' lives. She was right. I have always looked up to her, her strength, her disciplined studious nature, and her unbelievable belief that I could be successful in whatever I choose to do in life.

Indeed, Delynn is successful in her chosen career as a wealth manager and financial planner. However, like most beginning insurance agents, the start of her career was a bit rocky. In her first year, when she was struggling to make her first sale, her mother taught her a very important lesson about confidence. Elaine took Delynn to lunch and then across the street to a car dealership. Delynn was excited, thinking her mother was about to help her purchase her first car. Delynn was feeling very good and relieved during the sales process until she and Elaine sat down with the finance guy. Elaine made it clear that Delynn would be purchasing this car on her own. Delynn said, "No cosign, no help with the down payment, nothing! I loved that first car, but mainly I was proud. Proud that I made enough sales every month (barely in some months) to pay my payments and proud to learn that sometimes if you want something bad enough or *have* to do something strong enough, you will make it happen." Delynn never forgot those lessons.

Today, Alexander Financial Services, a firm Delynn founded with her business partner and good friend Reena Bland, is one of the top wealth management practices in Northwestern Mutual. Delynn serves as the chief business development officer, and Reena—who previously had been a financial representative and field director with Northwestern Mutual—is the chief financial officer. They have a professional team of five associates: director of investment services, director of investment operations, director of insurance operations and client service, director of operations, and director of planning. In addition, they have one other employee.

Delynn Dolan Alexander (right) and her business partner, Reena Bland.

## ONE OFFICE, FIVE YEARS, TEN BABIES

Delynn and Reena have been great business partners because they are friends first. (To learn more about how their partnership developed, read chapter 6.) In spite of the fact that they both have young children, they still work out together four days a week at 5:30 a.m. Maternity leave has been a way of life for their firm. From 2006 to 2011, the five members of their team had ten children. Juggling, although difficult, is something they all work on together and hold each other accountable for "if things get out of whack." The team members have a shared mantra of being "extremely focused on work when we are working and being home with our kids when we are home."

## GROWING THE BUSINESS AND EMBRACING CHANGE

Their success today is impressive: multiple Top of the Table (MDRT) qualifications and $1.5 million of annual revenue (and Delynn is only forty-four years old). As Delynn says, we are "well on our way to bigger numbers and so much fun with family, friends, and clients." Over the next five to ten years, they plan to grow their business in three ways:

1. Referrals to great people from our best clients (and sometimes from other clients)
2. Growth of existing clientele and peers' clientele through joint work
3. Mergers and acquisitions (acquiring new relationships from insurance professionals and investment advisors who have no one to transition their business to and providing holistic planning for the clients of other professionals)

Elaine taught Delynn about strength, discipline, and confidence. Delynn has learned those lessons well and has taken them a step forward by embracing all the changes in the industry to build a financial planning process that "clarifies our clients' goals and objectives for their financial future including planning for retirement, education, legacy, and philanthropy. Our analytics team assesses their insurance, investments, wills, trusts, and other assets. In collaboration with a client's legal and tax advisors, we advise our clients on their efficiencies to help make their goals a reality."

## OUT OF PERSONAL TRAGEDY COMES OPPORTUNITY

Ellie Mills (CLU, LUTCF, RFC, Ellie Mills Insurance Agency, Inc., State Farm) has been in the insurance industry since she was twenty-six years old. However, by that young age, she had already lived a lifetime, learning many difficult lessons. In 1983, when she was only eighteen and had been married four months, her husband was killed when their car was hit head-on by a drunk driver. She grew up quickly after that and is very grateful for three things that helped her put her life back together:

- health insurance
- auto insurance
- life insurance

As she recovered from the accident and the loss of her husband, she had no idea how her personal experience with these products would affect her career. In 1986, Ellie remarried and moved to Miami with her husband to open a nursery. In 1992, Hurricane Andrew destroyed the nursery and their home—but not her personal resolve:

> It was that event that catapulted me into the understanding that I was meant for [the insurance] business. It helped drive home what a noble profession it truly is and how we can make a profound difference in the lives of other people.

## DO NOT MISTAKE MY KINDNESS FOR WEAKNESS.

Ellie's early years in the business were not easy, although they could have been much worse if insurance had not helped her get on her feet—twice. By the time she entered the business, she and her husband were juggling children and careers. "There were days when it seemed impossible." When she had her second child, they hired live-in help to give them some relief from all their child care and home responsibilities. From those early days in the insurance business and a boss who said, "Sit down and shut up—you might learn something," Ellie has come a very long way.

Although she credits that gruff boss with teaching her how not to treat people, particularly subordinates, it was a veteran State Farm agent who became the most positive mentor of her success. He mentored her by example. Ellie respected him for who he was and how he grew his business:

> [He was] humble despite his incredible success ... He grew his business both inside and out, capitalizing on opportunities as they happened. He remained positive amidst industry and company changes, and led with a strong, compassionate demeanor. He helped others advance and grow when possible, but always kept the motto: Do not mistake my kindness for weakness.

In her early years in the business, she was determined to succeed because she realized she "loved doing this." She has never been a quitter and doesn't get discouraged easily. According to Ellie, "this is the only business where you can fail your way to success!"

Ellie Mills (in front of car, next to her name, in sunglasses) and nine members of the Mills Team preparing to participate in their community's annual Fourth of July parade.

In all of her successes in the industry, it is hard to find any failure, just lots of grit and determination. Today, she has two offices—each with a full sales and service team—and eighteen employees who offer ninety-six different products to their clients. Her business, which allowed her to achieve the 2013 WIFS Infinity Award for the highest income among WIFS Circle of Excellence qualifiers (qualification based on annual gross income), continues to flourish and grow. She and her colleagues work with poor as well as affluent clients. She describes her A-plus client as "one who cares about her or his family's financial future and is willing to take action to help protect and plan for it." There is no doubt that her passion comes out of personal tragedy and the miracle of insurance.

Ellie is pleased that her eldest daughter has entered the insurance business. She constantly tells her to get her profession started and under-way—and get her secondary education out of the way—before starting a family. While the business can be done with a family, it is easier once a solid foundation is established. Although the next five to ten years are slated to be her largest income-earning years before retirement—and she plans to maximize that growth—her primary goal is to help as many of her employees as possible put their names on the door of their own agencies. Four of her current team members are working toward this goal. Ellie knows she can't help others succeed in the business without continuing to grow as a leader. When asked how she can possibly juggle all the personal and professional parts of her life, she answers humbly:

> I continue to surround myself with individuals who help me with [balance] personally and professionally. I am extremely grateful for the point that I am in my life. I re-alize that while hard work and determination have had a part in getting me here, so, too, have the many wonderful people that have come into my life.

The four amazing women you have just met have achieved success in the financial services industry in very different ways. They have grown their businesses in a variety of companies and unique environments. All have struggled along the way, but they have never allowed their problems to interfere with their optimistic attitudes and commitment to their businesses—and, most importantly, their clients. They are women in a profession largely populated by men. Most of their managers have been male. They have worked with men who have lifted them up and been great role models. However, the opposite has also been true. They have sought to gather around them successful women and men who support each other. All of them are proud of being female and have utilized their unique traits and talents to seek positive mentors, professional peers, and clients who are willing to act on their advice. They are all team builders who treat their clients as friends and team members—not as customers. They are not afraid to laugh or cry with colleagues, employees, and clients. They all say loudly and with commitment, "I love what I do. I love my clients. I love helping others."

# CHAPTER 2

# GETTING STARTED

> At age thirty-two with two small children and both she and her husband in careers that did not compensate either of them for their time, talent, and education, Anne Franklin-Peiper decided that if they were ever going to be able to save any money, something had to change. "I didn't have a background in finance, business, or marketing," says Anne. "On a whim, I attended a workshop about women and money with my mother. The leader of the workshop was so compelling that I pursued an interview with her. I spent the interview trying to convince this woman why I could never work in sales. [She] saw something in me that I didn't see in myself. Because of this woman's vision and training, I have consistently been in the top 1 percent of producers in my office and among the top annuity producers in the company."
>
> —Anne Franklin-Peiper, CLU, ChFC, CASL, Wealth Management Advisor, Northwestern Mutual

## FAILURE WAS NOT AN OPTION

Most of the highly compensated female financial services professionals, including the women responding to the 2012 WIFS survey and interviewed for this book, started their careers shortly after college graduation. However, there are those who jumped into the career after marriage, children, and other jobs. For many of the women starting at older ages, something in their lives precipitated the need to make a change. For Anne Franklin-Peiper, it was fear that she and her family would never be able to save any money, her children would not be able to go to college, and she and her husband would not be able to retire.

Anne Franklin-Pieper (right) and her family.

For others, such as Kathleen Godfrey (Registered Investment Advisor, President and CEO, Godfrey Financial Associates), it was the unexpected death of her husband, being "suddenly single," that catapulted her into the business. Like Anne, Kathleen was in a job that provided her with neither financial security nor personal satisfaction. She, like Monica Jones, realized that as the sole supporter of her family, her salary was not enough for her two children to live the life she wanted for them. Likewise, her job would not give her the flexibility to be a part of their lives. Something had to change.

Kathleen Godfrey (right) and her two daughters at the New York Stock Exchange after the women of WIFS rang the opening bell, December 27, 2011.

Other very successful financial services women were dealing with life changes when they entered the profession. Robelynn Abadie was twenty-seven years old and divorced with two young children to support. "Looking back, [I was] pretty unsteady at the time. I cried a lot." But, Robelynn, like Ellie Mills who had lost her home and business in Hurricane Andrew, had no choice but to succeed. "Being driven to support my kids, I didn't have a fallback plan. I had to do it."

Some of the women featured in this book entered the career right after completing college. Barbara Brazda Dietze reports that her entry into the career was more by chance than a personally initiated job search. However, what she learned about the career during the interview process appealed to her.

> When I bought my first car after college, I met my car insurance agent who referred me to his friend, a sales manager at New York Life. Since I was unsure about what career path I wanted to take at this young age, I was convinced that the unlimited income potential and the flexibility to revolve my business around a family one day was a good fit for me. I learned much later [that] the deck was stacked against me as a young, single female who had no debt or family to support. I was driven by leading the office in group health insurance sales, which led me to working with closely held companies in the business market [in which] I thrive today.

With the help of her remarkable managing partner and mentor, Barbara did succeed. He saw something in her that led to her inclusion in a class and support group of fifteen young agents in her office. Barbara reports that one of her favorite sayings is "when the student is ready, the teacher arrives." She was ready. And lucky for her, her managing partner recognized this and provided her with the knowledge and supportive environment that led to her early success.

Barbara Brazda Dietze and Jim Adkins, Sr., her remarkable first managing partner, at her twentieth New York Life anniversary party.

## IF A FINANCIAL SERVICES CAREER IS SO TERRIFIC FOR WOMEN, WHERE ARE ALL THE WOMEN?

The Bureau of Labor Statistics, as quoted in a CFP® white paper, reports that 31 percent of all financial advisors are women,[12] a low number when you consider the much higher number of women in law, medicine, and accountancy. However, this percentage cited by this government agency seems high given the percentages of women that financial planning and wealth management corporations report having as representatives and planners. In a table titled "Gender Divide," appearing in the journal *Financial Planning* in June 2013, ten financial services companies, called the "Top Ten Firms," reported the percentage of women financial advisors in their field forces. The percentages ranged from a low of 9.94 percent in a large life insurance company that offers financial planning and wealth management to a high of 28.19 percent in a securities company. Four companies, all advisory, reported that their percentages of female financial advisors ranged from 12.78 to 16.71. Three of the ten companies appearing in the table did not provide data on the percentage of female as compared to male advisors.[13] Likewise a recent white paper

("Making More Room for Women in the Financial Planning Profession," Certified Financial Planner Board of Standards, 2014; used with permission) reported that a minority of 23 percent of all planners with a CFP® designation are women.[14]

Why is there such a large differential between the government agency's reporting of women in the profession and the self-reporting of companies and professional organizations? It could be that the Bureau of Labor Statistics' numbers represent financial services professionals as well as employees, including those who provide clerical assistance to professionals. However, whichever numbers are used, the government or self-reporting of corporations, the percentage of women in financial professions is significantly lower than the percentage of women in many other professions.

It is likely that this "feminine famine,"[15] a phrase coined in the CFP® white paper, is not only because fewer women than men join the industry but also because of what many of the successful financial services women who responded to the WIFS survey and participated in the interviews for this book call "the revolving door" of women entering and exiting the profession.

## LACK OF KNOWLEDGE ABOUT FINANCE, PRODUCTS, AND SERVICES MAY CREATE A REVOLVING DOOR FOR WOMEN

Unlike law, medicine, and accountancy, the professional education of most financial professionals begins on the day they enter the office or agency in which they plan to work. This lack of education prior to starting the career may be more difficult for women than for men. Recent studies of women consumers, as well as the data produced by the WIFS survey and interviews of women financial professionals, seem to show that women want to know as much as they can beforehand about a product they plan to buy or a career they plan to pursue.

The CFP® white paper reported that those women with or pursuing the CFP® designation had higher career satisfaction or greater optimism about the career than those without or not seeking the designation. The CFP® board's white paper commented that women seem to be more concerned with building credibility through education and professional designations than men.[16]

Kathleen Godfrey, a past president of WIFS and owner of Godfrey Financial Associates, in her WIFS interview said, "I strongly believe that the turnover rate in the financial services industry is shameful, especially in the insurance industry. People aren't given the necessary resources and support to succeed."

## CHUTES AND LADDERS: A CFP® WOMEN'S INITIATIVE RESEARCH STUDY

The CFP® white paper puts this in a slightly different way, but it arrives at the same conclusion, particularly when it comes to female recruits. Drawing an analogy to the children's board game *Chutes and Ladders*, the CFP® Women's Initiative (WIN) Advisory Panel—composed of primarily female financial services, marketing, education, and CFP® leaders—reviewed existing research literature on gender disparity in other professions to identify those chutes that can send women out of the financial services industry. We will examine these chutes and how they affected the women in the WIFS survey and those interviewed for this book in this and subsequent chapters.

## CHUTE # 1: "WOMEN, MORE SO THAN MEN, LACK ADEQUATE INFORMATION AS TO WHAT FINANCIAL PLANNING INVOLVES OR WHAT IT TAKES TO BE SUCCESSFUL AS A FINANCIAL PLANNER."[17]

A large majority of the women who responded to the WIFS survey—as well as those who participated in the in-depth interviews for this book—lacked financial education and sales training when they entered the profession. Although most have college degrees and many have graduate degrees, few of their degrees are directly related to risk management or financial planning. Some of the women in this study had the opportunity to intern in the industry prior to starting their careers, but this was the exception rather than the rule. Many commented that not being more knowledgeable about the industry, financial planning, and products created a large burden in their early years in the business.

When you couple this lack of information about financial services with women's desire for knowledge before they act, there is a serious disconnect between getting started quickly in the business and feeling confident in what she is expected to do. Toni Espey (CASL, Antonia C. Espey Insurance Agency, Inc., State Farm) now a successful agent and agency owner with State Farm in Florida, recalls that when the president of State Farm announced that the company wanted 10 percent of the agency force to become a CFP®, she decided to accept the opportunity and challenge. "It amounted to taking five to six courses, passing them successfully, and then sitting for a grueling ten-hour exam given over two days. Most of my friends turned down the challenge right away. I thought about it and decided maybe I could do it." It took her two years to complete the process. In the end, she was very proud of her accomplishment. And what she learned from the coursework helped make her feel confident in her ability to give good advice. "Women are different from men," she says. "We want to really understand the subject we are talking about. Men can talk about products that they don't understand and be okay with it. By passing the CFP® test, I knew I had the knowledge to help my clients with all of their planning!"

Juli McNeely (LUTCF, CFP®, CLU, Owner and President, McNeely Financial Services) is a successful financial planner and owner of her own company, and she is also the first female president of NAIFA (National Association of Insurance and Financial Advisors), the largest professional organization in the financial services industry. Juli remembers that her early years in the profession were made more difficult by her "fear." According to Juli, "I remember early on that I was so afraid that I wouldn't be able to answer everything for a client. I thought I needed to know everything before I could meet with clients. I was paralyzed by fear. I also had a lack of confidence in my own abilities. I second-guessed my decision [to enter the business] for several years before I finally started to believe I was good at being a financial planner and knew what I was doing." Juli credits the education and designations she sought and completed on her own and her involvement with other financial services professionals in organizations like NAIFA and WIFS for a great deal of her success.

Lisa Sappenfield Boyer (CFP®, Registered Principal and Investment Adviser Representative, Owner, Boyer and Sappenfield Investment Advisors, Transamerica Financial Advisors) says that her entree into the business is an interesting story. Her summer softball coach who was from a small town in Illinois became the first CFP® in Champaign County. He told her when she was a sophomore in high school that she could do what he did some day. She says that all she wanted in her high school years was to become a physical education teacher and coach, and she really did not know what her softball coach did anyway. However, around that same time, her PE teacher told her that the job potential for PE majors was low.

When Lisa started college, without really knowing what career direction she would take, she decided to major in her second career choice: business and finance. While in college, Lisa attended one of her softball coach's dinner seminars for prospects and clients. What he was doing looked like something she could do. "Within six months, I had started my career [as a financial planner] and have never looked back. I built my practice 'teaching' people about money and have actually coached sports most of those years as well."

Lisa Sappenfield Boyer coaching her girls' softball team.

Lack of knowledge leads to lack of confidence in advising clients, which leads to lack of income.

Although a very small percentage of women who completed the WIFS survey said that the training they received from their companies and agencies was inadequate, many commented anecdotally that there was too much to learn, too quickly, and too late. Their training was intense, and during that time, they had very little or no income. For most of these women, including those who are now top income earners, meeting with prospects prior to understanding what they were recommending was simply unacceptable.

Many reported that the early years were made even more difficult because money was always an issue. "I made no money the first three years of this business and actually lost a lot of money," says now successful State Farm business owner Toni Espey about her inauspicious start in the career.

Colleen Bowler (CFP® Lincoln Financial Advisors—Strategic Wealth Partners) is today the sole proprietor of the Strategic Wealth Partners in Dallas, Texas. She has been listed for several years by *D Magazine* as "One of the Best Financial Planners in Dallas." In 2012, she was Lincoln Financial Advisors' *Planner of the Year* in the Southern Region. She is also a member of *The Resource Group*, Lincoln's 175 top advisors. Each member of this elite group pays a fee for the privilege of working with other top advisors to increase their knowledge and provide better service and advice to their clients. That is today, but her early years were difficult and frustrating.

Colleen, like many of the women in this study, says that her start in the industry was not promising. "I started in this business by accident— going through a divorce while caring for a sick three-year-old (that I would become the sole parent of within a year)—and in need of a job. Friends said to me, 'You're good at math; you should talk to people that do financial planning.'" However, her knowledge of the industry and what financial planners do was very limited. According to Colleen, she made so little money in her first two years in the business that she "qualified for the [IRS] earned income credit."

## PREPROFESSIONAL EXPERIENCE IN THE INDUSTRY CAN LEAD TO EARLIER PROFESSIONAL SUCCESS

Some successful women in the financial services industry have found that a good way to overcome their fear of lack of knowledge as well as their concern about the poor earning potential in their first few years in the business is to work for others in the industry prior to starting their own businesses. Betty Harris Custer (CFP®, CRPC®, Founding Managing Partner Custer Financial Services, Lincoln Financial Advisors) had a fast and successful start in the industry in part because of experience she gained while in college and shortly afterward. "I started working my way through college as an office clerk for an insurance services office," says Betty. "When I went back to school I stayed on working and eventually became the office manager and training director. At age twenty-four, I started a financial planning firm with one of the older agents." Betty not only learned from her early clerical administrative work with this insurance office but also through her partnership, at a young age, with a much more experienced and senior agent.

Many women, writing anecdotal comments in the WIFS survey, report that they had various jobs in the industry prior to becoming professionals. These salaried jobs helped them gain knowledge and skills and overcome fear and lack of confidence. They served as receptionists in agencies, assistants to agents and financial planners, and office managers. According to one such woman, "I started as the receptionist at [a benefits firm] and am now the president/COO [of that firm]."

Some of the women served in supportive roles in the industry more than once. "I was lucky," reports one woman, "to have started in this business at age nineteen as a receptionist at a brokerage firm. When an opening for a sales assistant came available, I was able to take it, and from there I was offered a job as an associate consultant. However, I was not yet ready for the economic challenges [of the career]. My husband was in Iraq, and I lost my dad that year to cancer, so I left the business to stay home with my boys. I came back [two years later] as a registered assistant again, but the advisor I worked with needed a successor." She reports that her education, experience, and personality made becoming his successor "a great fit."

One woman, today a leading long-term care insurance specialist with a major insurance company and owner of her own company, reported anecdotally on the survey, "I nearly did not come back to the office after my training school. If it had not been for the respect I had for my manager, I would have bolted. What I did instead was come back and tell him that I wanted a salaried job in the agency for a few years while I learned the business, the products, and how best to advise people." Fortunately for her, he had a position as a recruiter and trainer open, and her prior experience in education was a good match. She took the job and agreed to entry-level compensation. She reports that doing so turned out to be a good decision. During the next eighteen months, "I learned the business, met with anyone and everyone who could advise and give me feedback, was licensed and credentialed, and had tons of prospects to call on before my first appointment to discuss long-term care. Consequently, I got off to a fast start, but I saw my income cut by more than half during the eighteen months it took to get up to speed, but it was all worth it in the end."

Women, more than men, may lack knowledge of finance and a career in financial services. However, those women who remain in the profession and succeed in the career cite education, training, and designations earned as being a significant component of their success and their ability to help their clients achieve financial security and independence. Although most of the women in the WIFS study did not major in fields related to their chosen profession (Robelynn Abadie majored in piano.), they rapidly sought ways to educate themselves. They did so by joining and actively participating in professional organizations and taking courses leading to professional designations. These women were attracted to positive, successful colleagues and sought mentors and coaches. If their companies, agencies, or managers did not provide the "ladders" they needed to lift themselves up and over the chutes that might defeat them, they found those ladders on their own. They persevered in spite of what may have seemed like insurmountable odds against them.

## CHUTE # 2: PREVALENT BUSINESS MODELS AND COMPENSATION STRUCTURES MAY BE UNFAIR AND UNATTRACTIVE TO WOMEN[18]

Many women in anecdotal responses to questions on the WIFS survey discussed how the financial model of income through commission only is a deterrent for entering the profession in the first place. For this reason, as stated previously, some of these women who ultimately desire a career in financial services will learn the business from other financial services professionals while being employed in the industry or elsewhere and earning a paycheck.

Several women commented that the nature of a financial services career, built on the value of helping others, is part and parcel to why starting in the business with limited knowledge and no salary is so repugnant. American women are typically the caregivers in their families for young children and for aging parents. Although juggling work and family will be discussed later in this book, earning an income or a second salary while raising children and taking care of parents and in-laws is essential to most families. If they are required to give advice or sell products in order to earn an income before they believe they know enough to do so, they fear they may be hurting their clients more than helping them.

It was difficult for many of the women in the WIFS study and interviews to earn an income while getting started in the business, and the business models and compensation structures of the companies or agencies where they began their careers did not fit their images of who they wanted to become and how they wanted to help their clients succeed financially. Couple this with what many women viewed as a climate of lack of support for the caring of children while working, and it is easy to understand why many women exit the career prior to knowing the benefits it could offer them and their families. Almost all of the women interviewed for this book consider a balanced life to be a successful life. If work is demanding too much from life and is not providing the income needed to support themselves and their families, leaving the industry might appear to be the women's only choice.

One female manager in a large insurance company reported on the WIFS survey that she knew she needed to change some of her recruiting language when a new female insurance agent approached her on the day of the first commission run after her contracting. "Where is my paycheck?" she asked, "I need it to buy groceries for my family." This manager immediately knew that if she were going to retain this female recruit, she was going to have to find a way to provide her with some compensation while she was learning the business. Compensation while learning the business is not the traditional model in an industry where commission is earned for products sold, and fees are earned for advice given or wealth managed. This compensation model can be an inherent difficulty for women who are more likely than men to be uncomfortable meeting with prospects or clients, giving advice, or closing a sale before they know enough to answer the difficult questions they might be asked.

Several women, including those in management and leadership positions, said anonymously on the WIFS survey that recruiting and retaining women of all ages will continue to be very difficult unless companies within the financial services industry, particularly insurance companies, figure out how to fairly compensate new agents while they are learning the business. Likewise, these women say, until companies, agencies, and managers determine that it is acceptable for a woman's career path to differ from a man's as she has and raises her children, women will continue to leave the career because they cannot meet the demands of high activity and earn a reasonable income at a time when their children need them at home. Many of the young women responding to the WIFS survey started in the industry when they were single; some had incredibly successful starts to their financial services careers. However, now that these young women are married and considering starting families, they reported worrying about the time they must take away from their office and clients while having children and raising them. And at the same time, they feel guilty because the demands of their jobs rob them of time with their children. If companies and managers do not work with these young women to help them find an appropriate balance, many will be forced to leave the profession.

## SUCCESSFUL WOMEN OVERCAME THE PREVALENT BUSINESS MODELS AND COMPENSATION STRUCTURES OF THE INDUSTRY

As previously discussed, many of the women interviewed for this book who have become incredibly successful in the financial services profession did so as suddenly single mothers. Others were leaving less lucrative careers and had little savings and few prospects for success in a business about which they had limited knowledge. Colleen Bowler, who started the business as a soon-to-be single mom of a sick three-year-old, comments about the financial difficulties of getting started: "I think in the early years, the highs and lows of commissions were very difficult to manage. Cash flow modeling sucked." However, these women overcame all of these obstacles. And perhaps because they could not afford to fail, they achieved remarkable success. They had to persevere.

One very successful young female financial representative and wealth manager for a large insurance company entered the business immediately after completing college at age twenty-two in 2002. She got married in 2013 and was pregnant with her first child when these interviews were conducted in 2014. Her company had recommended she participate in this study. She wrote in an e-mail to the authors of this book, "I am so sorry. I don't think I can help (with this study) for the next few months. I am having a baby in early June and slowly winding down." She spoke of her concerns about her ability to hold together her successful practice while being out of her office on maternity leave. "I hope," she concluded, "the initial questions I answered were of some use and I can be of help again in the future." Because this young woman had eleven years of experience prior to starting her family, had established herself with her clients and her company, and had a staff to help her through seven months when she did not work, she was able to resume her business, not quite at the level of her past success, but with every indication that it will continue to grow for many years in the future.

Ellie Mills began her career in the financial services industry when she was a young mother with children. Now her oldest daughter has entered the profession. Ellie says that she is constantly telling her daughter, "Don't do what I did." It is much easier to start the career when you are single, have completed your education, and do not have the responsibilities of a family.

Nicole Holland Hong, a successful young Northwestern Mutual financial representative, agrees with Ellie and credits her fast start in the career with being single and living at home with her parents. She says that living at home was very helpful in her early years. "I could focus on the career without the financial stress." She was also able to save quite a bit of money that she "invested" in her business and, eventually, in herself.

Many of the women interviewed for this book learned hard lessons about the business in their early years. If they had not had the personal fortitude to believe in themselves and keep moving forward, they may have joined other women exiting the revolving door.

Kathleen Godfrey was contracted with an independent broker-dealer during her first eighteen months in the business. Six months into the relationship, she realized that the branch manager for her broker-dealer had a serious substance abuse problem. "Frequently, paperwork was lost or mishandled; client checks went missing." During that same period, Kathleen was an independent life insurance broker contracted with a brokerage general agency. She was on her own, and no one had ever told her that she was entitled to an expense reimbursement allowance from the general agent. He recognized her naiveté and never paid it to her. Kathleen says that as a single mom with two young children, she really needed the money—and the GA knew this. It was a hard lesson that cost her at least $10,000 over two years in lost revenue. Kathleen could not afford to fail, and she found another brokerage GA and moved forward. Shortly after this time, Kathleen transformed her business structure to an RIA (registered investment advisor). "I've never looked back. No way was I going to have my financial security jeopardized."

## FINANCIAL SERVICES COMPANIES AND FIELD MANAGEMENT CAN HELP WOMEN AVOID THE DREADED CHUTES AND REVOLVING DOORS

A high-level female field manager for one of the large insurance companies anonymously expressed concern about the training requirements and expectations placed on women by most of the other, primarily male, field managers in her company. She makes it clear that she strongly believes that female financial representatives must be "very focused and work hard," probably more so than men. She points out that the work-life balance within families is very complex and women's work can be hard on the family.

If a married woman with children is going to be successful in this business, she needs "a good support system that will allow her to grow." That support system needs to be "not only at home but also at work."

She is critical of her management colleagues—men and women—in her company and throughout the industry. "More women would be successful," she says, "if companies made them feel welcome." This includes such simple things as not requiring breakfast meetings when women are getting their children to school or evening training schools when women are home cooking for their families or attending their child's soccer match.

"Women need positive role models and mentors," she says, and other industry leaders agree. Sometimes providing role models and mentors can solve multiple issues. It is possible, for example, to match up new recruits with more experienced young professionals, including women who are raising families. The office support system might include strategies such as teaming a new recruit with the successful, young, soon-to-be mother and providing this new agent with compensation for the work she does with this woman's clients. The new agent acquires a successful female mentor as well as a small income, and the more senior financial professional gets the help she needs to service her clients while she is out of the office. Most importantly, a teaming relationship such as this provides both women with a better chance of long-term success.

Every situation is different, but some simple and some carefully thought-out strategies—with the goal of helping make everyone more successful—can create a welcoming office environment for all. This woman field manager says that she works together with everyone in her office, attempting to meet their unique needs. As many have said before, being in financial services "is a tough job." Women are different and have different needs. This does not mean, as the women in this study prove, that they will be any less successful than men. It simply means that the business models in which they are trained and the environments that allow them to grow must be supportive and welcoming to women as well as to men.

## MANAGEMENT CAN HELP WOMEN SUCCEED AT HOME AND AT WORK

As another woman responding to a survey question perceptively wrote, "Women are only successful if things are going well at home." Other women in anecdotal comments in the survey, including some in management, suggested that a different career track for women might make sense. Many women commented that they are willing to work as hard as, often harder than their male colleagues—but not on the same calendar.

When a woman is raising young children, partnering with other women or men and sharing jobs and clients might give her more flexibility to be with her children. She might share cases with young single male and female colleagues who can meet with clients during the evening hours when she needs to be home with her children. Managers can help pair women who have young children with successful senior partners who are willing to share business and potentially pursue succession. Working from home can be helpful to women when their children are young or have special needs. Women are often able to blend their family's lives with their businesses. There are women who have created successful practices by working with families with special needs children, for example. Other successful women have focused on providing financial advice for women in transition: divorce, death of spouse, remarriage, becoming a single parent, or caring for elderly family members.

If a woman enters the business with young children or becomes a mother within the first few years of starting in the business, partnering with a more experienced financial professional may make a world of sense in making both of them more successful. Because most women are strong relationship builders, the young mother in the partnership could be the professional who completes the fact-finders, develops the financial plans, and proposes a variety of solutions. She can be the partner who attends luncheon meetings to network with other professionals. She may volunteer in the community to make the business more visible while providing an important service. She can also speak with the contacts she is making to get referrals for the partnership. Of course, she can also meet with clients. She will know many other young mothers with whom she can meet during daytime hours. These kinds of partnerships allow each partner to share her or his strengths, leverage time, make it possible for both to spend more time with family, and help grow the practice of both professionals. If the partnership is successful, it may continue for many years as the business grows and flourishes. Managers can encourage these types of partnerships and provide leadership for them.

One woman described her career track by saying, "I worked very hard when I was able. Meaning, while I was young and had no other responsibilities other than myself—I worked. Even after I got married and started a family, I was at work when I was at work, and I was at home when I was at home. I am present wherever I am at the moment. It makes me a better business owner, planner, and mom."

## HIGH EXPECTATIONS ARE IMPORTANT FOR WOMEN AND MEN, BUT DIFFERENCES IN HOW THEY WORK NEED TO BE CONSIDERED

Although women need to be as accountable as men and managers' expectations of women's work as rigorous, how women do their work might differ and therefore require management to rethink some of what is measured. For example, the number of appointments in a day or the number of applications written in a week in the early years in the business can be a good indicator of future success for a man as well as a woman. However, there are other important elements of a financial professional's work that might also be important indicators of future success, particularly in an era when many of the most highly compensated professionals are comprehensive financial planners.

Women, as reported by every woman in this study, are relationship builders. They tend to have long appointments with clients, get a great deal of information from them, and propose many solutions. Therefore the number and quality of in-depth fact-finders and financial plans done with prospects and clients might be an important indicator of the future success of a woman. Since women tend to build long-term relationships, measuring the number of contacts a woman has with a prospect or a client may also be a good indicator of future success. The successful women in this study make frequent client contact an important part of their business plans.

The successful women in both the WIFS survey and interviewed for this book report that they have built their practices on referrals. They also indicate that they are reluctant to ask for referrals before the client knows the quality of the work that they do. Once that occurs, they ask, expect, and even require referrals. Therefore, it is important for management to help women network and develop relationships quickly so that they are comfortable asking for referrals. The number of referrals women get and how quickly they develop sources for referrals are critical to their future success.

In partnership relationships, such as those discussed above, expectations will need to be set based on what each partner is expected to contribute to the partnership. Both are expected to contribute equally, however, what they contribute may differ considerably. It will be important for the partners and management to work together to establish expectations and measure their success.

## WOMEN PRACTITIONERS DESCRIBE WHAT MAKES A COMPANY GREAT

Women who report on finding the great companies, and many do, talk about the number of female leaders in the company. They discuss the company as working for them, not vice versa. Here is what some of the women say about the great companies with whom they work: They "inspire you to view this career as part of your life and instill in you to help people, one at a time, by impacting them in a positive way." These companies have a culture in which "it takes a village to grow a representative" or a financial planner.

Many of the survey respondents and women interviewed for this book have found that the best way to have a great company with a female-friendly environment that puts clients first is to grow it themselves, establishing their own business identities, teams, and offices. Sadly, one woman commented, "The industry still has a locker room feel." Companies can support women as they mature in the business by providing successful role models of other financial services professionals who have established their own businesses and offices. Corporate leadership can develop templates of best practices for starting a business and opening an office, providing the women with the knowledge, information, and support they need to help their new businesses thrive and grow into incredibly successful practices that can become models for others and be sustained into the next generation.

Although all the women interviewed discussed the wonderful, kind men who were patient mentors as they grew in the business, they all also commented that too many of their male colleagues did not meet their ethical expectations of how to work with clients, and they preferred not to work with these male colleagues. For these successful women, success is not about the amount of money they make; success comes only when they make a difference in the lives of their clients and find a balance in their own lives. This balance allows them to love the work they do for others in the financial realm but also love being a mom, a wife, a friend, a caregiver, and someone who gives back the gifts she has been given. Great managers and great companies help women and men achieve success on the highest and most ethical plains.

## CHUTE # 3: GENDER BIAS AND DISCRIMINATION MAY KEEP WOMEN OUT OF FINANCIAL SERVICES[19]

Gender bias, as suggested above, may be ingrained in some financial service business models. Women may be treated as naïve, as Kathleen Godfrey was. Or they may be held to higher standards or expectations than their male counterparts. Their agencies, companies, or offices may not be welcoming or female friendly. And their success may be measured based on criteria that are not appropriate given the needs, traits, and strengths of women.

Women were asked on the WIFS survey, "Do you feel it is more difficult for women to succeed in the financial services industry?" The lower the income of the female respondent, the more likely she was to respond "yes." Nearly 50 percent of all women earning under $500,000 per year responded that it is more difficult for women to succeed, whereas only a third of the respondents earning more than $500,000 per year answered in the affirmative. Does this mean that successful women experienced less gender bias and discrimination or simply that it is more obvious to the women who are, perhaps, younger and less financially successful? Both are probably true.

The CFP® white paper reports similar differences in how CFPs and non-CFPs respond to questions about whether men or women are more likely to be successful in the profession. According to WIN (Women's Initiative of the CFP Board) survey data, 31 percent of the CFP® professional community believes that "women are more likely than men to have what it takes to be great financial planners."[20] While 46 percent of the women in this community "are even more strongly convinced of their gender advantage over men," only 9 percent of the financial advisor community as a whole believes "women have the edge over men as successful financial planners."[21] When this same question was asked to officials of financial services firms, according to the CFP® white paper, only 7 percent voted for women as most likely to be successful in the profession; 41 percent voted for men. However, when these same firm officials were asked about specific qualifications important in financial planning, such as "are well trained by educational programs" and "are strongly ethical," they gave the advantage to women over men for all five qualifications and by more than twenty percentage points in three.[22]

Even though a large percentage of CFP® professionals believe that women make better financial advisors than men and financial services firm officials acknowledge that a large percentage of women financial advisors have a higher level of skills than men, there is still the predominant belief that men are more likely to be hired as financial planners than women. Likewise, 54 percent of men and 60 percent of women believe that "the office culture in financial firms makes men financial planners feel welcome and respected." While 48 percent of men believe the culture is equally welcoming to women, only 29 percent of women agree.[23]

One of the very successful women interviewed for this book remembers how a difficult pregnancy with triplets, early in her career, nearly shot her out of the business. Not surprisingly, this pregnancy was a very difficult and emotional time for her. It also was a pivotal moment in her career:

> I was a high-risk pregnancy and actually lost the little girl at nineteen weeks. [Twin sons were born early, but in good health.] I was in and out of hospitals for about

four months. During that time, I was still working from the phone, and my staff would bring me any paperwork I needed to look at or follow up on. I was home from the hospital, still pregnant, and my manager came over to talk to me. He explained that his boss [a woman] had asked him to tell me that since I wasn't in the office because I was on bed rest, they were going stop me from writing any new business and limit my office to servicing existing clients. Once my manager told me they were going to shut my agency down, I explained that I knew of another agent who was sick.

He had been in a terrible accident that left him in a nursing home with limited cognitive ability. His agency, only a short distance from her agency remained open. She told her manager that he could keep her from doing any new business, but she would be hiring a lawyer—and his boss could discuss with that lawyer why she was not shutting down the agency of a male agent with brain damage, but was of a female agent with a high-risk pregnancy. She says that she learned a lot about a business model that at that time had managers of both genders treat men and women differently. More importantly, she learned about her own strength and her ability to make this career work for her.

Although women responding to both the WIFS survey and being interviewed for this book acknowledge that they have experienced gender bias and discrimination, they also have found ways to overcome it. Many report being the only woman in their offices or agencies in their early years in the business. Those who remained in the business found ways to compete and succeed in a male-dominated culture—but sometimes at a price too high to pay.

Pamela Gilmour (CPA, CFP®, CLU, ChFC, CASL, Financial Planner and Owner, Financial Fitness, Guardian Life Insurance Company of America) is today a detached (not in an agency or company office) Guardian agent doing business as Financial Fitness. She remembers her early years in the business positively, but she also recognizes that being one of the very few women in the office and her drive to succeed were both costly:

From years four through twelve, I worked in a very successful, upbeat Guardian agency. The GA (general agent) was a unique individual who could both lead and manage a large group of entrepreneurs. He exposed us to great inspiring speakers, systems, and encouraged us to work with one another. There were very few woman producers in the agency (less than 5 percent), and many didn't stay for long. I was one of the guys and felt respected by the GA, producers, and administrative staff. Failure was not in my vocabulary. I was driven toward success versus fear. I wanted to help as many people as I could and assumed that would lead to abundant compensation and independence. It all worked.

Today Pamela Gilmour still competes, but now in charitable, athletic endeavors such as this race for the Alzheimer's Association.

Pamela also comments about how being "driven" in the early years in the business had personal consequences. "I did not do a good job of balancing my personal life with my new position, and it resulted in a divorce. I was so focused on succeeding and outproducing my male counterparts that I became a workaholic." Today Pamela advises other women financial services professionals to set priorities and "make your personal life and that of your family number one." Pamela and most of the other women entrepreneurs interviewed for this book have found significant satisfaction and their greatest success in their own offices away from corporate and agency male-dominated cultures.

≈

Successful women, including those featured in this book, overcame the obstacles they found getting started in the financial services industry by

- searching for great companies, agencies, or offices with many female leaders and an environment that encourages the personal and professional growth of women and men;
- seeking a supportive manager who is concerned about her personal needs and helping her succeed while meeting those needs;
- establishing personal and professional support systems at home and at work;
- getting as much education and training as quickly as possible, even prior to actually starting in the career;
- building relationships with successful colleagues with similar values systems;
- partnering with other agents, representatives, and planners so that the woman and her partners can achieve a balanced life;
- finding mentors and ethical colleagues with whom to work;
- seeking a positive, nurturing work environment even if it meant establishing her own; and
- persevering, but not being afraid to make changes if necessary for professional growth and life balance.

# CHAPTER 3

# TRANSCENDENT MOMENTS

> I was looking to improve my career opportunities, having completed my CLU, ChFC, GAMA training, and achieved MDRT. I visited a "top manager" in Kansas City, who looked over my resume and then asked, "Do you type?" I knew then that if I was going to achieve my goals, it would be strictly up to me!
>
> —Donna A. Patton, CLU, ChFC, Registered Representative, Financial Advisor, Principal Financial Group

## TRANSCENDENT MOMENT: DEFINED

A transcendent moment is an instant in time when something happens that changes the direction of your life. It may be, like Donna Patton's, an "ah-ha," an otherwise unremarkable event or comment that dictates what she must do. The same comment from the same manager could also be the chute that sends a less self-confident woman out of the business—the straw that broke the camel's back.

## TRANSCENDENT MOMENTS IMPACT CAREERS

Many women in both the anecdotal comments on the WIFS survey and the in-depth interviews for this book report how these unexpected moments affected their careers. Toni Espey remembers an incident that at first made her angry but then made her think. She was twenty-six years old, new to the business, and working in a two-agent State Farm office. She was in a life insurance training class. A man in the class was discussing how to determine how much life insurance a person needs. Here's what Toni says about the incident:

> He looked at me and asked, "How much money do you see yourself making ten years from now?" Before I could open my mouth, he said, "$40,000?" He then proceeded to work his numbers. I was stunned that he didn't give me a chance to answer. Then I became a little bit angry. *How dare he think that I'll only make $40,000? What gives him the right to think that's all I am worth?* So I asked myself that same question that night and decided that I wanted to make a goal of earning $100,000 a year before I turned thirty. I did accomplish that goal in my thirtieth year, and I credit that rude man who wouldn't wait for my answer!

Transcendent moments may not lead to immediate action, but they may be the force that makes eventual action inevitable. The tragic death of Ellie Mills's first husband in an automobile accident did not immediately lead her to a career in insurance. However, their accident and his death made Ellie aware of how important auto, health, and life insurance were to reconstructing her broken life.

Ellie's subsequent life events of losing her home and her nursery business in a hurricane were enough to make her rethink her life and pay attention to what she had learned several years earlier. Again, Ellie saw how insurance made her and her family's lives whole again. She finally sat up, took notice, and realized that helping others manage these risks was what she must do.

For many women who participated in the interviews for this book, death or divorce made it necessary to find a career that would compensate them well and give them the flexibility they needed to be a part of their children's lives. Being suddenly single, particularly if there are children, requires many life adjustments. Robelynn Abadie and Colleen Bowler were both divorced mothers when they entered the financial services business. Both of them said that they never intended to become financial planners and did nothing to prepare for the career. But suddenly single with young children, they needed jobs—and failure was not an option.

Colleen comments that the first few years in financial services were really difficult:

> [The business] requires a lot of upfront work, continual learning not only in the financial area but in relationships, with complexities and challenges abounding ... That said, I can't imagine a better job to have as a parent. I was able to arrange my appointments to be at school during parent read time. [I was able to] be on all the Boy Scout campouts and to spend two weeks every year my son was in high school handling the food for ninety kids who were performing in a musical. This business has given me the flexibility every parent needs (let alone a single parent). I have been able to get up early and work, and work after putting my son to bed. I was able to make the income that paid for him to go to college, fund my retirement, and pay the salaries of my staff. And who better to care for clients than one who knows how important a family is to have around them?

Kathleen Godfrey and Monica Jones were single mothers after their husbands died unexpectedly at young ages. Kathleen's early years in the career were made more difficult because of her decision to have her business remain totally independent, rather than signing "a career contract with either an insurance company or investment brokerage wire-house." As Kathleen points out, "I had to seek out *all* training on my own." She also had to find an insurance brokerage company and a broker-dealer to help her place her business. Inexperience and, by her own admission, naiveté led her to trust people who were unstable and dishonest. This cost her precious time and thousands of dollars in expense reimbursements to which she was entitled but not paid. However, Kathleen, like all of the other successful women in this book, took these hard lessons, learned from them, and turned them into the building blocks of her career. She makes it clear, she had only two choices: "(a) succeed or (b) go on welfare." Today, she works with only successful, honest professionals and has many professional relationships that are advantageous to her and, most importantly, her clients: a CFP® on retainer and written contracts with a CPA, estate planning attorney, and P and C (property and casualty) insurance specialist.

Monica Jones and her daughter celebrate Monica's success.

## LIFE'S TRAGIC EVENTS MAY CAUSE US TO CHANGE OUR BUSINESS MODEL

At times, life tragedies and familial responsibilities take women away from their work. However, for strong, confident women, these difficult personal experiences eventually provide the incentive they need to move their careers to new levels. Gail Linn (CFP®, CASL, ChFC, LUTCF, Financial Services Representative, Financial Planner, MetLife Premier Client Group of NYC) reports on a series of events that literally took her out of the business. In 1999, her mother fell out of bed. The fall resulted in major back surgery, and the surgery caused complications that required additional stomach surgery and landed her mother in intensive care.

Things were touch and go at the hospital, but she pulled through and was transferred after four weeks to a rehab facility where she stayed for eight weeks. She eventually came home where I orchestrated home health care for eight months until my brother and I decided to relocate her to an assisted living facility near him in Northern Virginia.

Not surprisingly, Gail's insurance production during this period was very limited, and she was told that she would be terminated from the company unless it improved. Given the time she was spending caring for her mother, she knew this would be impossible. So she sought a salaried position within the company and was hired as a MetLife trainer educating new advisors. "At that time, the company allowed me to retain my book of business."

To service her clients, Gail partnered with another female advisor. She says of her time as a trainer, "I gained tremendous experience speaking in front of groups." Her position also gave her the opportunity to share her experience as an advisor with new recruits and help them build their careers.

Gail turned what could have been a career-ending experience into an opportunity. After eighteen months as a trainer, she transitioned back to the field, moved her office from Brooklyn to Manhattan, and set her sights on a new target market: corporate executives and professionals. Since that time in 2002, her business has grown dramatically. Her experience with her mother also taught her about the importance of a product she had previously known little about: long-term care insurance. She had also learned that planning for the risk of chronic illness or injury is important for everyone. Today, she educates her clients, particularly women, about that need.

My mom's experience taught me a lot about the need to plan and the value of staying positive. I'm able to share this experience and the lessons I've learned from it with my clients and prospects and help them make good decisions when planning their own futures.

On the day Gail Linn closed on the purchase of in her new apartment with a view of Manhattan, she said, "An achievement of my twenty-five-year career—it took me that long to get this!"

Perhaps it is because these women could not afford to fail that they have become so successful, in terms of what they earn and, more importantly, the clients they have influenced and helped.

Kathleen Godfrey said, "I try not to think of what could have, would have, or should have happened. For a long time, I believed my learning curve would have been shorter and less steep if I'd signed a career contract [with a financial services company]. In the end, I wouldn't trade my experiences with anyone."

## TRANSCENDENCE MAY ALSO COME FROM THE JOYS IN OUR LIVES

For Kathleen Godfrey, her husband's death might have been what cata-pulted her into the business, but the other transcending moment in her life occurred many years later. In 2007, she was awarded the Woman of Excellence award by the Albany Chamber of Commerce:

> It's a really, really big deal. You're featured in the local newspaper, interviewed on TV, and there's a standing-room-only luncheon to honor the winner. I flew in my eighty-five-year-old mother from Buffalo to attend, and she sat with my daughters in a ballroom of 650 people, all there to honor me! It was a very proud moment.

And for Kathleen and many of her female counterparts in the indus-try, those proud moments are also important events in the lives of their businesses. Since that time, Kathleen has continued to receive honors and recognitions. Another proud moment occurred in 2014 when she was named Woman of the Year by Women in Insurance and Financial Services (WIFS).

Many of the women interviewed for this book discuss how earning a designation, like CFP® (Certified Financial Planner), receiving a ma-jor award (like Robelynn Abadie's 2010 Woman of Excellence/Business Category Award by the Louisiana Women's Legislative Caucus), or be-coming the president of a national organization (such as Juli McNeely, current and first female president of NAIFA) catapults their business to a new level. These accomplishments are moments of joy for the woman as well as a transcending moment for her business.

And because so many of the women choose to give so much of their time to volunteerism, charity, and philanthropy, these recognitions build their reputations in their communities and their businesses. Likewise their volunteer work and leadership in the financial services industry builds national, international, and local recognition. Robelynn has served as president of two national professional organizations: WIFS and Association of Health Insurance Advisors (AHIA), as well as one international organization: the Million Dollar Round Table (MDRT) Foundation.

Juli McNeely's installation as the first female president of NAIFA, 2014.

Betty Harris Custer was fortunate to have early years in the business that were "filled with success and achievement and support." For many years, Betty has been extremely involved in her community, and today, she spends as many as twenty hours per week serving on nonprofit boards and working for these charities. Although she has never been National Agent of the year, she does not regret her decision to focus on community service and her family as well as her business. She is content with being in the top fifty of five thousand Lincoln planners. Through the work she has done in her community and the recognition she has received for that work, she has built a business that has helped thousands of clients reach their financial goals and allowed numerous young financial planners to thrive and achieve success.

## THE WORST DAYS IN OUR BUSINESS MAY LEAD TO OUR GREATEST SUCCESS

For some women, being told that they can't ensures that they can. Anne Machesky, a very successful financial planner at Sagemark Consulting/ Lincoln Financial Advisors, recalls an early day in her career when a manager told her she would never make it in the business. His comments were enough to make her want to prove him wrong, and, indeed, he was very wrong.

Certainly Gail Linn and some of the other successful women featured in the book agree that the day they were told they were about to lose their contracts qualifies as one of their worst days in the business. All of them, in different ways, overcame this seemingly impossible hurdle to achieve significant success.

Paula Zonin with her father and her first and most important mentor.

Paula Zonin (CLU, ChFC, LUTCF), a very successful Vice President, Brokerage Manager, and Disability Income Specialist at National Financial Network, LLC, a general agency of the Guardian Life Insurance Company of America, remembers a fateful day when it appeared her career was ending just as she was beginning to experience success. In 2001, Berkshire Life, the company she represented as her father had before her, announced they were merging with Guardian Life. "This knocked me for a loop," says Paula. "However, it was a blessing in disguise. Guardian Life Insurance had a premier DI (disability income) product, and marketing [it] to brokers became a job I loved." For some women, a forced change of direction can lead to increased success if approached with an open mind and a belief that failure is not an option.

Delynn Dolan Alexander grew up with a single mother who was a successful insurance agent for Northwestern Mutual. By all accounts, Delynn was destined for success and leadership within the company. Delynn spent her early years as an agent in the same agency as her mother in Dallas. She got off to a fast start and was quickly identified as a future field leader. In order to pursue her dream of becoming a general agent (now called managing partner) for Northwestern, she moved to Chapel Hill, North Carolina, to become a district agent and build a new office in that university town. Her boss, the managing partner, was a few miles down the road in Raleigh. Delynn worked very hard and built a company-recognized internship program with students from numerous local colleges and universities. However, after five years in management, she and her managing partner mutually agreed that she would step down. According to Delynn:

> I had my sights set on someday being a managing partner and felt like my whole life's plans were crumbling away (at the old age of thirty-two). Having to reframe myself, my role, and my future was overwhelming and frightening. Looking back, this was one of the most important steps in where my career is today. Without this happening, I would have never had conversations with Reena [Reena Bland, Alexander Financial Services' cofounder] about leaving her practice and working together to break out and create a wealth management practice using tools of financial planning.

Delynn's five years of management experience provided her with knowledge and skills that have helped her grow and manage the company she and Reena continue to build. Those years taught her how to treat employees, team members, and partners so that all can achieve success and fulfillment. Delynn has also learned how to select the best members for her team. "As we've grown as a team, we try and ask ourselves [she and Reena], 'Can I laugh with this person? Can I cry with this person?' We will."

Delynn wonders how she had the strength to use what could have been a career-ending experience to move forward. Maybe it was her need to show her managing partner that she could succeed. She has, and she and that managing partner have developed mutual respect. Maybe it was her desire to be one of the leading financial planners in her agency and in the company. She is, and she speaks nationally to other Northwestern financial representatives about how she, Reena, and the rest of their team have built the business. But, more likely, it is her desire to help her clients, her team members, and other women in the business reach the goals they have set for themselves:

> We coach and mentor as a part of giving back to what got us here ... We also mentor and coach other women nationally as part of our goal to help women have a support team that may not exist in their local offices.

## LEARNING WHY WE DO WHAT WE DO MAY CREATE THE PASSION WE NEED TO DO MORE

Most of the women interviewed for this book came into the business with little knowledge of what it means to be in insurance and financial services. Some, like Ellie Mills and Monica Jones, had learned from experience about the importance of risk-based insurance products and good planning. However, it is often the experience of our clients that makes us passionate about the work we do.

Although Monica Jones had personal experience that taught her about the importance of life insurance, an experience with a client renewed her passion for the good the product can do:

I remember one occasion I met a young couple with three small children in my office. He worked in construction; she was a stay-at-home mom. He said to me, "Monica, I am young and healthy; nothing will happen to me." We spoke for another twenty minutes, and he finally agreed to get life insurance coverage. Three weeks later, a drunk driver hit him while he was driving home from work after a late shift. He was killed. I will never forget the moment when I came to his house with the check from his life insurance. His mother-in-law hugged me and called me "the family angel." This is what I do for a living, and I get paid for it. What a life!

Moments like these reinforce what successful women in financial services already know: what they do makes a positive difference in the lives of individuals, families, and businesses. And for all of the successful women interviewed for this book and responding to the 2012 WIFS survey, this is their most important motivator.

## SOMETIMES OUR ACTIONS CREATE OUR OWN TRANSCENDENT MOMENTS

There are probably almost no career financial services professionals, female or male, who would tell you the early years in this business were easy. Most report on the long hours, the steep learning curve, the rejection, the frustration when a case that was sold is declined either by the insurance company or the prospect, the volumes of paperwork, the lack of assistance, and little or no compensation for all of this work and frustration. In the worst cases, financial services professionals accumulate debt.

Juli McNeely, now president of NAIFA and owner of McNeely Financial Services, says, "Getting started in this industry is so difficult. I remember those early days well and truly felt I had made a mistake."

Why would anyone stay in the business? For many of the women in this study, it was their unmitigated belief in their future success and their willingness to fail in the small things to reach the goals they had set. Reaching their own goals, according to WIFS survey responses, is the biggest motivator toward women's future success. When things were the toughest, they sought inspiration to move on. All of them understood, even if they had helpful people around them, that ultimately they had to succeed on their own. So these successful women did things such as seeking out other like-minded professionals, either through professional organizations or their companies, as cheerleaders or mentors.

## ACTIVE INVOLVEMENT IN PROFESSIONAL ORGANIZATIONS CAN KEEP US ENGAGED IN OUR BUSINESSES

Juli McNeely gained much knowledge and experience through her work in NAIFA. Through the contacts she made in NAIFA and MDRT, she became a member of an all-female study group of women financial services professionals that meet each year at MDRT and in another nonprofessional location. According to Juli, "They have become a huge asset to me professionally and personally." They keep in touch via phone and have hired a business coach to keep them on track. (You can read more about coaching in chapter 5.)

Most of the women interviewed for this book belong to several professional organizations. Often they found these organizations early in their careers. Some were introduced to the organization by a respected colleague or manager, but more often, they sought them out themselves. The organizations provided them with knowledge about the financial services profession and helped them make lifelong contacts with other professionals, some who had already achieved tremendous success and others with whom they shared the same dreams, problems, and goals. Their involvement in these organizations often did more—it provided the transcendent moments that kept them moving their businesses to new levels, often when they were most vulnerable.

Robelynn Abadie was very lonely in her early career days in Baton Rouge, Louisiana, where there were only two other female agents. Robelynn reports that both of these women were pioneers in the industry, much older than she, and had no time for a new female agent. Fortunately, her first career agency manager was a caring, patient man who saw her great potential. He was not disappointed. Robelynn became the top-producing agent in the office by the end of her first year in the business. Although she is convinced her manager often did not know what to do with her, he took her to her first NALU (National Association of Life Underwriters; now NAIFA) meeting. He got her involved in committee work immediately. She says, "I didn't know the significance of this at the time."

The most important outcome of her involvement in NALU is that it put her in contact with other female agents through WLUC (Women Life Underwriter's Conference of NALU, now WIFS, an independent national organization devoted to women in the industry). She attended her first NALU national conference because she learned that there was to be a WLUC organizational meeting at the conference—and anyone interested in a female support group was encouraged to attend. She reports that she went to that meeting but was intimidated by the women there. According to Robelynn, "I nearly went home the next day ... those women really intimidated me. Most were from the Northeast and were unlike any women I had ever met in a business or professional role. *Tough*. I was still this naïve, young southern girl."

Robelynn Abadie with career legends and role models Bill Walker, Woody Woodson [Mrs. Woodson also pictured], and Charlie Flowers in the early days of her career.

The following day, as she was planning her departure, she met two women who invited her to dinner, so she canceled her plans to leave the meeting and stayed to attend the dinner. Billie Root Coburn and Lorna Venderbush became her lifelong friends and were her mentors for nearly a decade. They introduced her to MDRT and gave her the successful female role models she had been seeking. She became a charter member of WLUC and a regional vice president. When WIFS became an independent organization, Robelynn became the national president and continues today as an active member of WIFS.

Barbara Brazda Dietze, with her mentor Diane Gould, at New York Life's 150th anniversary celebration. [Diane Gould, Barbara Brazda Dietze, and Lady Liberty]

Like Robelynn, Barbara Brazda Dietze was introduced to MDRT by her mentor Diane Gould. Barbara was pregnant with her second son when Diane invited her to breakfast in 1993 and gave her a pin that said *MDRT in Dallas*. Diane told Barbara that she needed to qualify for MDRT that year (not an easy task) and attend the MDRT meeting in Dallas that June. Barbara did both. According to Barbara, that transcendent moment changed her life.

> [At the MDRT meeting] I met incredibly successful, caring, giving financial advisors from different companies all around the world. I volunteered and quickly became involved in leadership ... I have not missed a meeting since 1994 and have now qualified for MDRT Top of the Table (today requiring approximately $1,000,000 in annual insurance or financial services production) five times.

Lisa Sappenfield Boyer cites two different organizations as being important to her development as a successful financial planner and businesswoman. Her broker-dealer is Transamerica Financial Advisors. Like many insurance and investment companies, Transamerica has a top producers' group of which Lisa is an active member. Not only is she a member; she was the first and only female president of the board, chosen by the past presidents and current board members. In addition to this being an achievement and an honor, her involvement with this group has helped her grow her business.

Lisa's work with WIFS has also been important to her growth as a financial services professional. Currently, she works with Transamerica to help lead the company's group of WIFS members. This group of women meets annually at the WIFS national conference. Through her work with WIFS and her broker-dealer, Lisa has grown as a professional and has gained skills and knowledge that have made her a better businesswoman and financial advisor. Likewise, she is now personally rewarded by helping other young women find their own transcendent moments so that they can grow in the financial services profession and provide important knowledge and service to their clients.

Gail Linn's first involvement with a professional organization was with NAIFA. It was at NAIFA local chapter meetings that she met other professionals in the business and learned the importance of professional education and designations. Through her involvement with NAIFA, she completed her LUTCF (Life Underwriter Training Council Fellow) designation. What she learned about products through the coursework for the LUTCF and the confidence this knowledge gave her helped make the early difficult years in the business less difficult. Gail, like so many other successful women in the financial services industry, reports that the lack of female role models in the industry in the 1990s encouraged her to seek out women in professional organizations.

Gail was the only female in her MetLife office of fifteen representatives. In fact, she says, there were very few women in the entire region. So Gail joined together with ten women to form the Brooklyn Region Professional Women's Group with the goal of educating other women about finances and insurance. These ten women worked together to offer seminars at a variety of venues. "Through this experience," says Gail, "I found my voice and realized that this (financial services) was my passion."

At an educational seminar at a hospital women's center in Staten Island, New York, where Gail and two other women were presenting, one of the audience members asked if any of them held a CFP®. This question moved Gail to pursue her CFP® designation. She recognized the importance of this designation in gaining credibility with an audience.

A colleague encouraged Gail to attend an MDRT annual conference in 2004. She has not missed one since. It is from this organization, she says, that she gains a global perspective of the business and has met some of the best practitioners in the industry. In addition, the inspirational messages from the main stage speakers encourage "me to do my best for my clients and continue to grow my business." Today, Gail has made a commitment to help younger women in the industry achieve their potential by getting involved with WIFS for support and mentorship. For her work in and service to the industry, Gail was awarded the WIFS Angel Award in 2014.

Ginger Weiss (Senior Partner, Creative Financial Group; Registered Representative, MetLife Securities) credits a MDRT meeting early in her career as the transcendent moment that may have kept her in the business:

> I attended my first MDRT after one year in my business in 1983. I was inspired by so many of the attendees and platform speakers. I believe that experience was what truly made me commit to this career.

Today, as a senior partner and leading financial planner, Ginger still regularly attends MDRT and NAIFA meetings, in addition to her company leaders' meetings.

Nancy Wolfe-Smith started with State Farm in 1987, "right out of college." Like some of her other successful female peers, she spent twelve of her first sixteen years in leadership within the company, learning the business before building her own business. For eight of those years, she was training in the field. She left corporate leadership in 2005 to start her own agency and gain more personal freedom. She has grown her business, becoming the WIFS Platinum (highest income earning) Award winner.

Nancy is an active member of NAIFA and WIFS and currently serves as a national board member of WIFS. She cites these organizations as helping her develop field leadership skills and providing "a view of the world outside of State Farm." She encourages the members of her office team to actively participate in professional organizations and seek education. She is a good role model for them. She is active on boards and participates in several professional study groups, giving her the opportunity to share and receive ideas. She says it is through these associations that she has learned ways to provide positive feedback to her employees, leading to professional and personal growth for them as well as for her.

For many of the successful women responding to the WIFS survey and interviewed for this book, WIFS has provided them with female role models, mentors and mentees, study groups, and lifelong friendships. Kathleen Godfrey, a WIFS past president who owns an independent RIA (Registered Investment Advisor) business, says, "I couldn't have succeeded without WIFS. I learned that there were others like me who were 'in the trenches' and I could pick up the phone and get help, empathy, and friendship."

Donna Patton (CLU, ChFC), a registered representative with the Principal Financial Group, echoes this sentiment. There were few female mentors or role models in her early days in the business. "Mainly," she says, "it was my friends in WIFS who provided encouragement and support." Donna also served as a president of WIFS.

Pamela Gilmour is a past national board member of WIFS. However, for the growth of her business, her most important contribution to WIFS was starting a local WIFS chapter in Baltimore, her hometown. The chapter now has forty-five members, and Pamela currently serves as the president. According to Pamela:

> I am very committed to helping women be successful in the financial services industry, and my passion and energy for this organization (WIFS) is contagious. I have been the membership chair on the national WIFS board and have been positively impacted by working with other like-minded women to take that organization to the next level. In these women-centered associations, I have found the support, camaraderie, and knowledge that have been critical in growing my practice.

≈

Transcendent moments experienced by these women include personal tragedies, moments of joy and accomplishment, and moments they created for themselves. It is these transcendent moments, whether tragic or joyous, that got them into the business and helped keep them in the business and moving forward along their path to professional success. Why? These women learn from all of the moments in their lives, and they persevere. Neither people nor events can sway them from the professional path they have chosen. This does not mean they have not changed course when necessary to do so, but it does mean that they have utilized even the unexpected and unpleasant bumps in the road as learning and building experiences.

# CHAPTER 4
# JUGGLING, BALANCING, AND BLENDING

> My husband is a grain farmer who never complained about being alone with our children in the evenings during those first ten years, so I could go on appointments. I did not go to an office five days a week until my youngest of three was in first grade. He also supported my passion for coaching sports because he knew that filled my soul and made me happy. I am a master of time management and calendars, along with the fact that I only require six hours of sleep a day.
>
> —Lisa Sappenfield Boyer, CFP® Reregistered Principal, Investment Advisor Representative, Boyer and Sappenfield Investment Advisors, Transamerica Financial Advisors

## SUCCESSFUL WOMEN BALANCE CAREER, MARRIAGE, AND MOTHERHOOD

Juggling, keeping many balls in the air at the same time, is an image women have used since the 1970s to refer to their lives as "working women" who are also mothers, wives, coaches, friends, teachers, and team players. They are arbiters of ethics and etiquette—and all the other things women do to keep themselves and their families healthy, happy, and fed.

The term juggling was probably coined by Letitia Baldrige in her 1976 book: *Juggling: The Art of Balancing Marriage, Motherhood, and a Career.*[24] There was no better woman to define this term than Tish Baldrige. Born in 1926 to a Nebraska congressman father and a mother who would sacrifice anything to educate and nurture their three children, Tish attended the best private schools and universities in the United States and abroad.

Her mother, in an era when most women worked in the home, believed the education of her daughter was every bit as important as the education of her two sons. After graduation from Vassar and graduate school in France, Tish began her career in a less than auspicious way. She, like most young women in the early 1950s, was unable to land the jobs that young men—with far fewer credentials—were able to get with ease.

On the advice of a personnel officer at the State Department's Office of Foreign Service, she took a secretarial course for two months and was able to get a job as the social secretary to Evangeline Bruce, the wife of the US ambassador to France, David Bruce. Evangeline recognized that Tish's intelligence and knowledge of the French language would make her invaluable to the Bruces' post in France. It was through this job that Tish gained what she called "first-rate training in diplomatic logistics, the science of protocol, and the art of social power play." It was the networking she had done, the diplomatic skills she learned in France, her smattering of Italian, and her ability to type that got her hired, sight unseen, by Clare Booth Luce, the first woman ever appointed US ambassador to a major foreign power.

Tish's job was to assist in the communications of an embassy where the staff spoke no English; at that point, the ambassador and her husband (Henry Luce, publisher of Time, Inc.) spoke no Italian. This job and the connections it provided put Tish in a position to be offered a job as the first female executive and head of public relations of Tiffany's, the country's leading jewelry firm. This job led her to her appointment as Jacqueline Bouvier Kennedy's social secretary during her and President John F. Kennedy's years in the White House. From there, she took the advice of the president's father Joseph Kennedy and took a position with the Kennedy-owned Merchandise Mart in Chicago. It was there, as well as in her years at Tiffany's and in the White House that she learned the furniture and design industry. And when she opened her own public relations company, Letitia Baldrige Enterprises, her first clients were Sears, a Chicago institution, and the Chicago Merchandise Mart.

It wasn't until Tish was in her thirties that she married Robert Hollensteiner. According to Tish, their marriage surprised everyone. For Tish, like many of the women in this study, her marriage and their two children changed everything. Now she was the owner of a new company, a wife, and the mother of a son and a daughter. Tish began to learn the true art of juggling when each of her children was born "at the end of a full workday." Her maternity leave consisted of three weeks for her first child and two for her second.

Many years later, Letitia Baldrige wrote the autobiographical book *Juggling*. She also wrote numerous other autobiographical and manners books, making her best known as an arbiter of social graces, hospitality, and etiquette. Throughout Tish's life (she died in 2012), she gracefully and with great humor juggled her own life, the lives of her family, and the lives of her employers. In addition to authoring many books in the last two decades of her life, she became an important philanthropist and volunteer, impacting the lives, particularly through educational opportunities, of future generations. The women featured in this book may be made from the same mold as Letitia Baldrige, but they have found that juggling and balancing are not what they need to do to make their lives whole. Instead they must *blend* and make all aspects of their lives one: children, spouses, other family members, team members, and their businesses.

## THE BLENDED LIFE: WORK AND LIFE ARE ONE

The term *juggling* has negative connotations for many successful professional women today. Most would agree that early in her career, particularly when a spouse and children first entered her life, she had to juggle. It was important to figure out how to keep all the important elements of her life moving in sequence. However, as she matured, she began to recognize the danger of juggling. If many elements are juggled at the same time, it is possible for one or more of these life elements to fall out of place—and all could tumble.

The very successful women interviewed for this book love what they do professionally and recognize the importance of their work in the lives of their clients. But above all else, they value their families. And they are committed to the service they provide to charities, their communities, their companies, and their profession. It is simply unthinkable that one element of their lives falling out of sequence could jeopardize the rest.

Therefore, successful professional women today, who learned from the pioneering professional women who preceded them, move as quickly as possible from juggling to *blending* (or integrating) all parts of their lives into one.

In a video interview for ForbesBrandVoice, Northwestern MutualVoice,[25] Delynn Dolan Alexander said, "My work is my life; it is who I am … I *love* (emphasis provided by Delynn) what I do. And being a mom is who I am. It is not that they are mutually exclusive. It is who I am. I am one person. So it is important for me to blend in; instead of separate, I integrate."

How has she accomplished this? She and her business partner, Reena Bland, have been in their own offices since they founded their business prior to having children. In the early days of their business, they each worked between fifty and eighty hours per week. As Delynn says, "There was certainly nothing we had to juggle." They both agree that working so hard at the start of their company was an advantage.

Then the babies were born. Delynn, Reena, and other members of the team had ten babies in five years. They had to find a way to integrate their children into their work lives. They did, and they still do. Delynn reports that when the babies were small, they were often in the office being held by Mommy or Daddy as she or he made phone calls. If something else had to be done, there was always someone else available to hold the baby.

Delynn says that she wants her children involved in her work life because she loves her work and recognizes its importance to others. It is good for the children to learn these values early. Delynn's children, Reena's children, and the children of their team members are included in their workdays as much as possible. As the children get older, each of the partners and team members has a home team and a home support system for caring for the children. However, the home teams and the work team are integrated. Delynn says that one of the ways she accomplishes this is by keeping only one calendar that includes her professional appointments and her family appointments. She and her other team members also work from home when necessary (technology has made this easy). They keep business hours that allow them to be home with their families every evening and on weekends. When they travel to company or industry meetings, they include their families whenever possible. According to Delynn, neither she nor Reena attempt to have it all.

> Instead of a balanced life, we focus on leading a blended life so that there isn't a true separation between our families and our careers. We have our careers so that we can have our families, and we have our families so that we can have our careers.

By shifting the focus from juggling (or balancing) to blending, Delynn and the other successful women featured in this book are able to move from what's impossible to what's possible. According to Cali Williams Yost, a flexible workplace strategy expert and author of the book *Tweak It: Make What Matters to You Happen Every Day*, "When you focus on balance … all anyone focuses on is what they don't have, because balance does not exist."[26]

## BLENDING ALLOWS WOMEN IN THE FINANCIAL SERVICES INDUSTRY TO CONTRIBUTE TO THE LIVES OF OTHERS

Although the women who participated in the WIFS survey and were interviewed for this book have very different jobs in the same industry, all of them agree that the most important thing about what they do, what they love the most, is their ability to influence the financial lives of their clients, their clients' families, and their clients' businesses. Being able to positively impact the lives of their clients as well as the lives of their own children and other family members is why they juggle, attempt to balance, and eventually blend all the important things in their own lives. Of the women interviewed for this book, eighteen of twenty-three have children. Today, these children range in age from two to forty-five. Nine of these women already had one or more children when they entered the profession. Some had spouses who could help with the children; others were widowed or divorced. In addition, these women—like Lisa Sappenfield Boyer—coach, volunteer, hold important leadership positions in many organizations and in their companies, take care of elderly parents, assist spouses in their businesses, mentor new financial representatives, and do countless other important things that make their communities better places to live and work. And these women are the CEOs of their own businesses. They run businesses that train, promote, and pay the salaries of large numbers of team members who make it possible for these women to do all they do. How did they do it? How did they achieve so much, help so many others, provide a living for so many families, and have a quality of life that allows them and their families to thrive?

Lisa Sappenfield Boyer (center) with her team, including her son and partner Stan Boyer (rear).

## BLENDING A CAREER IN FINANCIAL SERVICES, FAMILY, AND A PERSONAL LIFE IS NOT EASY, BUT IT IS WORTH IT!

No disagreement here. A financial services career, particularly in the early years, is not easy. Perhaps that is why so few people pursue it and stick with it and the potential compensation is so significant. However, the women responding to the WIFS survey and interviewed for this book also agree that the hard work of the early years definitely paid off. It paid off in terms of the incomes they earn and in the quality of life and work satisfaction they experience. As one of the women responding to the survey said, "I feel blessed to have had the opportunity to do this job, to make a difference in the lives of so many!"

In the early years of the business, these women worked long, hard hours. Those with children worked late into the night after they put their children to bed, and again in the morning before getting the children out of bed and off to daycare or school. Work was calling on prospects, attending networking events, giving seminars, and meeting with clients during the day. In the evening, women with children used the hours while the children slept to make phone calls, do paperwork, and study for designations. And for those who could, usually because they did not have children or had a supportive spouse who would care for the children, evening work also included client appointments.

During the day, all these women report being fully engaged talking and meeting with clients and prospects. Lunches were often with clients or at professional meetings. Early mornings, usually before six, might include exercise, inspirational reading, and chores to get the children off to school and the workday started. Life was full and very busy.

When at home with their families, these women report that they were fully engaged there as well. All these very successful women with children discuss how important their time with their children was to them. Many of them entered this career because of the flexible schedule it provided, allowing them to be at their children's activities and at home when the children needed them. How did they do this? They all say that they were focused, wasted little time, and were fully present whether at home or at work. As Monica Jones says, "One of the most important things I do is I close the door at home when I leave, and I close the door at work when I leave."

All of these women have developed significant organizational skills and are good time managers. Routines are important, and environments are orderly. Robelynn Abadie reiterates what many of these successful financial services professionals said, "I do keep lists and enjoy marking things off. I established certain routines, and my kids were 'put' to bed by nine. That gave me time to read, study, or relax."

## IS DIFFICULTY IN ACHIEVING A WORK-LIFE BALANCE A POSSIBLE CHUTE FOR EXITING THE BUSINESS?

Although the Women's Initiative (WIN) CFP® study (*Making More Room for Women in the Financial Planning Profession*, Certified Financial Planner Board of Standards) hypothesized that the inability to juggle work, family, and fun would be a deterrent for women entering the financial services industry or seeking a CFP® designation, they found the opposite. When surveyed, both men and women ranked the issue of life balance as a relatively minor concern when considering the industry. In fact, many women (most in their twenties) who were participating in CFP-board registered educational programs told focus groups organized for the study that the flexibility and personal freedom of the job was a major reason for considering the career. On the other hand, many leaders in the industry still have the impression that women will exit the career when they start families.

But if women are generally not worried that they can manage their work, family, and personal commitments and still be successful financial planners, they have reason for concern that employers may see things differently. Women, men, the financial advisor community, and financial services firms are all much more reluctant to hire women as financial planners because of concerns that they will leave to start families than to believe the same holds true for men. (*Findings from the WIN Research*, 2014, 25–26)

The WIN research does not address the number of women who do exit the career when beginning a family, but it looks at the perception of women and men that the balancing act is not a particularly difficult problem. Women participating in the WIFS survey and interviews, all of whom are already in the industry, recognize that balancing is not easy, particularly in the early years of the career. They also make it clear that some of their difficulty in juggling is due to business models that are not female friendly (i.e., management expectations that they will attend early morning meetings or hold evening appointments).

All of the successful women (as determined by income) responding to the WIFS survey and those participating in the in-depth interviews for this book found ways to overcome these problems. All of these women had a strong belief in their ability to succeed in the business and a commitment to being there for their clients. They were not thwarted by unreasonable demands or what others thought of them. Robelynn Abadie recalls, "I never worked at night. I was told I couldn't succeed if I didn't, but for me, that wasn't an option ... I had to find daytime activity, so I jumped out into the business market early on."

## A WOMAN'S INABILITY TO BALANCE WORK AND LIFE MAY NOT BE HER FAULT

The businesswomen who participated in various phases of the WIFS study frequently mentioned the revolving door of women entering and exiting the financial services industry, particularly insurance. In most cases, these women did not view the inability of the women to balance life and work as the issue that caused them to leave the industry. Many indicated that they believed that there were many reasons for the women's premature departures (lack of belief in self, lack of commitment to the career, unwillingness to work as hard as necessary, etc.).

However, at the same time, these women agreed that too often managers at all levels within the industry were not as supportive or helpful to new female recruits, particularly those with children, as they could have been. The young women were not recognized by management for their achievements as their male counterparts were. Some of the successful women in these studies laugh at what they call the "stupid mistakes" of their managers, things such as giving a very small woman an extra large golf jacket to reward her for reaching "his production goals" at a male-oriented event that she could not attend because her children were not included. While this may be humorous, and all of us can envision the drama as it plays out, it is also symbolic of the lack of management commitment and belief in the young women they recruit and train (as documented in the CFP® study findings). This is a large part of the reason why many of the women interviewed for this book say that the best thing they ever did to blend their careers, families, and lives was leaving corporate or agency offices and opening their own. For many of these women, this is when their businesses began to soar.

## SUPPORT TEAMS AT HOME AND AT WORK ARE ESSENTIAL

Of the top income earners responding to the WIFS survey, half hired their first staff person in their first year in the business, and 52 percent of the women with annual incomes over $200,000 hired staff by their third year in the business. Because money in the early years is tight, hiring staff early is one of the ways these women demonstrated their belief in themselves and their long-term commitment to their careers. Hiring and training a support team is also how these women were able to focus their efforts on what they do best: prospecting, networking, and developing long-term client relationships. As Barbara Brazda Dietze says, "I was convinced early in my career to hire a full-time assistant. I was spending time doing two jobs as my own assistant and as a financial advisor and was better off spending my time doing the latter and hiring a suitable person to fill the [assistant] role."

Most of the highly successful women responding to the survey and interviewed for the book, particularly those with children, discussed the necessity of having support and help at home as well as at work. Delynn Dolan Alexander gives this advice to new financial representatives:

> Find a network of support. If these people are not in your office, that's fine. But have them and make arrangements to check in daily/weekly. You will need folks you can laugh with in this business and those you can cry with. Life is crazy and so is this business.

Because Delynn, Reena, and the other young professionals on their team have so many young children, they all recognize that things happen. They know there will be days when a team member will need to remain home to take care of a sick child or will need to leave the office early to deal with the frequent small emergencies that are a part of family life. Sometimes, Delynn says, it might be necessary for a team member to work after hours or at home. "So, we arm our team with Internet and iPads and make it happen."

Delynn Dolan Alexander and her husband with their two young children.

Reena Bland, Delynn's business partner, with her husband and two young children.

Many of the women interviewed for this book credit their husbands with providing the support at home that allowed them to focus on work while at work. According to Lisa Sappenfield Boyer, "I couldn't have succeeded in this business without the support of my husband, and my personal discipline. We had three children in the first six years of my practice."

Nancy Wolfe-Smith echoes Lisa's appreciation. She says of her husband, "He has always been very supportive of my career." One of the small things he did to help Nancy succeed was being available to pick up their child each day after school.

Robelynn Abadie was single for her first fifteen years in the business. When she remarried, she also increased the number of her children from two (hers) to five (theirs) between the ages of nine and nineteen. Her children were the oldest; her husband had a nine-year-old son who moved in with them. He also had "two girls who lived with their mother, but were back and forth." According to Robelynn, "It took some kind of juggling to stay focused." However, she also points out that "just being married and having a husband was very different, as far as routines. No question, I married a guy who understood (somewhat in the beginning) what I did, how I was dedicated to the industry and not just my business. He never got in the way of my pursuit of those quests."

Monica Jones has also happily remarried. She says of her husband, "He is my rock." There is no doubt that the importance of a supportive spouse or partner cannot be overestimated.

All of the successful women with children comment that their children were also important members of the home support team. Betty Harris Custer says that her husband and children have understood that as a business owner, she can't totally leave her work behind for evenings, weekends, and vacations. "Long ago," she says, "I realized that checking in a few times daily and then putting work out of my mind was easier than trying to be totally isolated." Although she did check her messages most days, her children were always her priority. "I always said I never wanted my children to view their mother as the picture on the wall. Attending their events was always a priority in my scheduling, and now my grandchildren are." Betty's husband joined her in the business shortly after the birth of their second child. From that time forward he and Betty partnered in the workload at the firm and at home.

Ellie Mills makes it clear that it takes an entire family, a village, to provide the support that allows these entrepreneurial women to build their businesses. Ellie said in a written interview for this book, "And, I would be remiss if I did not mention my beautiful family who cheered me on from the beginning: my husband, two daughters, mom, dad, brother, and a plethora of dear friends who continue to encourage me to this day."

Betty Harris Custer with her son, husband, son-in-law, daughter, and three beautiful grandchildren.

For Lisa Sappenfield Boyer, the ultimate confirmation of her children's support of her in the business is the success each has achieved in their own professional lives. Particularly gratifying is that her son, Stan, is now an investment advisor working with his mom.

Barbara Brazda Dietze says of her twenty-three-year-old son, "To my astonishment, he recently made the decision to pursue a career in the financial services industry. All of those years of living and breathing the business and attempts to have a positive impact on my family must have made an impression."

Scheduling, as Betty mentions, is critically important to all of these women. Although it is impossible to schedule for the small (or large) emergencies of life, it is possible to schedule and important to make children's field trips and sporting, music, dance, and other events priorities on the calendar.

Barbara Brazda Dietze agrees, "I sought a career that could revolve around marriage and children. I was determined to be available to my children, even as a mother with a career. I didn't allow interference while at work that would delay or detain me from parental obligations included in my day." Barbara, like many of the other women featured in this book, was able to achieve this balance between family and work with the help of "a very supportive spouse and when the children were younger, an extremely dependable and loving nanny."

Robelynn Abadie concurs with all of the women who appreciate the career for giving them the flexibility to spend time with their children. "One of the things I loved most about my career was that if I organized my time and appointments well, I had time to spend with the kids at their ballgames, dance recitals, track meets, twirling, cheerleading, music lesson ... you name it; they did it. It gave me immense enjoyment that I was able to participate in their lives and not as a casual observer."

## SUCCESSFUL FEMALE FINANCIAL SERVICES PROFESSIONALS VIEW CAREER AND LIFE AS ONE

Several of the women commented that during the years their children were young, they gave themselves permission to work at their businesses part-time. Knowing that what they put into the businesses is what they get out of the businesses, they look at their careers as a whole. For those who did not have children in the early years of their businesses, these were the years they focused primarily on work. Then while building their families, their focus shifted primarily to their children. They recognized that as their children became more independent, their career focus would shift back again to building their businesses. They acknowledge that thinking of the career in this way may have meant that it took them longer to build their businesses, but it also allowed them to live all parts of their lives to the fullest. Paula Zonin comments:

Becoming a mom really made my career something I focused on only part-time. This is a business that what you put into it, is what you will get out of it. At the same time, it enabled me to earn a nice living on my own schedule. What would seem like crazy hours to some worked well for me. I think this is a great business for any woman who wants a career and family.

Lisa Sappenfield Boyer agrees. She tells the young women, some daughters of her colleagues whom she mentors, "It is okay for it to take longer in years to achieve a certain status if you are happy with work and family and know how to have fun!" She says of her work with these young women, "If they are a mom, then I reassure them that with balance they should *not* have guilt. I can tell if they really have a passion for the business, and if they do, I assure them how much they are needed by their current and future clients."

## FINDING A PERSONAL VILLAGE IS CRITICALLY IMPORTANT TO ALL OF THESE SUCCESSFUL WOMEN

Many of the successful financial services professionals in this study had to find support systems in ways they might not have imagined. Ellie Mills and her husband both had businesses. So when their second child was born, they hired live-in help to allow them to keep up with both their family and business responsibilities. For many, who do not have spouses or other family members who can provide child care, a nanny is not only an employee—but a valued member of the family team. Many women find that hiring excellent household support is as important as having a support team in the office. Household support team members include those doing child care, cleaning, yard care, and regular maintenance work. Most of the women who commented about their household support teams look at the salaries paid to them in the same way as they view the salaries paid to their in-office team and staff members: an expense of doing business. One of the respondents to the survey commented that the IRS might not consider her home team as a business expense, but she does. Her home team includes a housekeeper, a landscaper, a pool service, a handyman, and numerous other "helpers" as often as they are needed. Without them, she says, "I could not run my business."

## OTHERS FIND SUPPORT IN THEIR COMMUNITIES

Robelynn Abadie, as a single mother, needed an extensive support system. She found her answer in her church.

> The church I joined in Baton Rouge had a private school, so I enrolled the kids there. There was an after-school program to 6:00 p.m. and also summer day camps. Our church was our life in many ways, and we were on that campus almost seven days a week. Keeping them in school, regardless of the expense, gave me peace of mind. The people knew us well, so if I was running late, I could just call and someone would be helpful.

Toni Espey, the mother of twin boys and a younger girl, says that when her children were very young, she could take them to the office with her. She worked independently, and her clients enjoyed seeing her children there. Eventually, her husband quit his job to stay home with the children. Although Andy was making more than she was at the time, they recognized the potential was in her job. Now that their children are grown, Andy works with her, and they hope that one day one or more of their children will join them in the business.

For a number of these women, it made more sense for their husbands to stay at home with the children while they went to the office to run the businesses. Anne Franklin-Peiper's husband is a stay-at-home dad for their two children. Having him at home has made a huge impact on her business because she can devote full-time to it without worrying about the day-to-day needs of her children. And she says the family has more resources now than ever before.

Toni Espey's clients were well aware that her family was important to her because they saw her interacting with her children in the office. And Toni reports, they respected the commitment she had to her family.

Even though Andy Espey was the children's primary caregiver, there were times when he needed Toni's help caring for the children so he could accomplish other important tasks.

Toni Espey and her family at work.

Ginger Weiss reports that she told her clients that her children were her priority. According to Ginger, because of this, her clients have been very respectful of her time and have arranged their schedules so they can meet with her during the day. On the rare occasion when a daytime appointment has not been possible, Ginger has turned the client over to someone else in her agency who can go to an evening appointment. So in this way, she has made other agents part of her support team. The commitment these women have to their children—as evidenced by the children being blended into their work lives—serves as a good model for their clients. Since the business of these women is helping build the financial security of families, seeing the female professional as a loving mother is a great way to reinforce the client's commitment to her or his children. That can't be bad for business!

Ginger Weiss with four of her six grandchildren.

## EMBRACING TECHNOLOGY CAN MAKE THE JOB EASIER

Many of the women in the survey and the interviews mention technology as a member of their team. As Delynn Dolan Alexander said, iPads, e-mail, and the Internet allow her team members to work from wherever they are needed, including from home. Although all the women recognize the importance of the personal touch, they also know that time on the phone playing phone tag with clients and prospects can be reduced by using technology effectively. Technology can make it possible for these women to be in more than one place at a time. While meeting with a client, another client may be reading an e-mail newsletter the financial advisor sent, and prospects may be viewing her website to determine if she is the kind of person with whom they want to work. Many of these successful women have team members who focus, at least in part, on maximizing the effective use of technology in their practices. Others have hired technology coaches.

Imagine the advantage these successful women have today as compared to Tish Baldrige and other career women of the 1960s and 1970s. As several of these successful female financial services professionals pointed out, they can be home with a sick child while meeting with a client via a webinar or conference call. While they are meeting with the client, other clients, prospects, and team members are sending e-mails they can respond to later. At the same time, social media (primarily LinkedIn), business websites, and the Internet are silently working on their behalf. Of course, this requires coordination and oversight, but this can be accomplished on a flexible schedule by their team members.

## WHAT ABOUT ME?

When you are so busy and your days have too few hours for all you hope to accomplish with many demands on your time, it is hard to add anything else to your schedule. However, every woman in this study knows that something else must be added—and that is *me time*. What that means is different for each woman, but all agree that time for themselves is critically important if life is to remain balanced and blended. Many of the women in the study say that one of their biggest regrets is not learning how to take care of themselves sooner.

Most of the women in this study admit that balancing their personal and professional lives is not always easy, even if they have been in the business for many years. In fact, Anne Machesky admits that she has not done well balancing her own life. "I am dedicated to my business and various committees 24-7," she says.

Ellie Mills says that sometimes that balance "comes in and out of focus for me depending on what's happening in the business." However, she says that she continues to surround herself with friends and family who help her balance her life both personally and professionally.

Delynn Dolan Alexander also points out that having a network of support will help you balance your life. Donna Patton says that at the beginning of every year, she and her husband work on the balance between their personal lives and her business by planning their yearly calendar and agreeing on vacation dates and other plans.

Barbara Brazda Dietze obtains balance in her life by "trial and error and open dialogue with family and business associates." Nicole Holland Hong says that she sets priorities for her personal and business lives and goes public with them. "By going public, it keeps me in check and allows others to hold me accountable when I need it the most."

Other women find that the only way to blend business and personal lives into one life is to *get out of the office.* Betty Harris Custer and her husband, who is in the business with her, have had a cabin three hours away from their home and business for the past twelve years. At home, life is focused on family and work. But the cabin, Betty reports, "is a place to focus on us." Betty also makes time for her adult children and grandchildren. She travels to San Francisco frequently to help her daughter care for her five-year-old son and five-month-old twin boys.

Donna Patton with her family.

Many of the successful women in the WIFS study, particularly those who have been in the business for many years, have been able to shorten their workdays or workweeks and take more and longer vacations. Kathleen Godfrey reports that in recent years, she has had a four-day workweek and takes regular vacations. She also quips that her kids have forgiven her for the early days of her business when she was a single mom, working so hard that she often was forced to miss their track meets. Today Kathleen and her two daughters take "awesome trips together." She looks forward to her daughter Molly who graduated from college with a degree in finance in 2014 joining her at Godfrey Financial Associates at the end of 2015. Molly spent a year "cutting her teeth" elsewhere in the financial services industry before joining her mother's company.

Pamela Gilmour blends business, fitness, and relationships.

A number of the women in the study talk about how important exercise is in their blended lives. Pamela Gilmour is so committed to the importance of physical fitness, her own and her clients, that she has named her company Financial Fitness. If you go to her website, you see the merging of her two passions: fitness and finance. The photo on her homepage is of Pamela and her two associates on exercise bikes. For years, Pamela has combined her love of exercise and athletics with her commitment to local charities. She raises money by running, including $31,000 for completing four half marathons over a four-year period for the Baltimore Alzheimer's Association. Pamela, who was president of the local Executive Women's Golf League, has also chaired a golf tournament for Boy Scouts and raised $10,000. She says of her well-balanced career and personal life today:

> After twenty-five years in the business, I have created great balance between my personal and professional life.

I do not arrive in the office before 10:00 a.m., [before then] I am either at the gym or at home with my forever fiancé, enjoying the morning. My staff arrives at 8:30 a.m. and stays until 5:00 p.m. or later if in a client meeting. We try not to schedule [regular] client meetings on Mondays or Fridays, have a team meeting every Monday, and vendor meetings and special client meetings on Fridays. Between Memorial Day and Labor Day, the staff can leave at noon on Fridays if their work is done.

Toni Espey, like Pamela, focuses on her physical fitness through her sport of choice: tennis. She says she wishes she had invested more in herself earlier in her career. Today, after she takes her twelve-year-old daughter to school, Toni heads to the tennis courts. She tries to play every morning and typically gets to her office around noon. She says that she can do this because she "empowers her staff to do most of the selling themselves." Andy, her husband, who stayed at home with their three children while they were young, now works with Toni in her office. According to Toni, he is her partner at work and still supports her in her dreams.

Monica Jones, who is still relatively new to the business, learned the importance of *me time* early in her work life. She says that she schedules an hour of *Monica's time* every day. She uses her time for many things. Sometimes she spends it with her daughter, her husband, or friends. Other times, she uses it to run errands. She says that her Monica's time allows her to keep on top of things in her personal and family life as well as in her business. According to Monica, if you can stay on top of everything, you will be successful.

Although not all of the women interviewed for this book have achieved what they consider to be a perfectly balanced life, they all strive to find that balance. And the juggling they still must do has become easier as they have matured in the business. Most of them have found that blending the most important aspects of their lives makes it possible to juggle new things as they come along. And new things will come, professionally and personally. Over time, they will determine if this new element of their lives is something that should be blended in or can be dropped without threatening the blended life they have worked so hard to achieve.

—

The nature of the financial services business requires a great deal of *up-front effort*: finding prospects, meeting with prospects, and turning them into long-term clients. In addition, the learning curve in the early years is very steep and demands significant time and effort. As the woman's business matures, much of the hard work she did in the early years of her business now allows her the flexibility to choose the clients with whom she will work. The relationship she has with these clients, the advice she has given them and they have taken, and their trust in her and her team make it possible to begin each year with a client base that will provide her an ongoing income as she continues to grow her business.

Although the business she does with these clients may become more and more complex, it is also more satisfying, and in many ways, it is easier to close. In addition, her partners and professional associates now assume many of the responsibilities that were hers in the early years of her practice. And her staff takes on important tasks that free up her time to do what she does best: meet new people, work with existing clients to help them grow and transfer their wealth, and manage the business so that it can grow and everyone can prosper. All of this gives her more time for the other important things in her life: family, friends, community, volunteerism, and herself. This is why all of these women say, "I love this career."

# CHAPTER 5
# BECOMING A FINANCIAL PROFESSIONAL

I am the second planner in a three-generational organization. My son joined the firm, initially as an intern and then as a planner in 2012. My mother, a pioneer in her organization, started the firm and obtained her CFP® in 1985, long before it was fashionable for a woman to pursue financial planning professional education.

I would not be in this business without my mother's guidance. She is first and always my leading role model. Most of what I know, I learned from her. She formulated techniques for working with men, based on her knowledge of how differently men and women think. She modeled the art of negotiation, and when she was right about an issue, she generally prevailed. There were numerous times when men in the organization attempted to discount her role and avoid compensating her fairly, all under the guise of its only "business."

A leader in her area of expertise, she sat on the agency management team. Male agents referred to her as the "gal" in business meetings. She gently requested they not address her in that manner. She demanded equal treatment. I miss her to this day. Had I not worked with her for eight years prior to her premature death, I believe I could never have achieved the independence I now enjoy or cope with the constant stream of changes we adjust to every day.

—Melanie Shanty, CRPC®, R.S.S. Financial
Services, Inc., Lincoln Financial Advisors

## THE FINANCIAL SERVICES BUSINESS IS MOST OFTEN ENTREPRENEURIAL

Although the careers of the successful financial services professionals featured in this book and responding to the 2012 WIFS survey vary significantly, there is one very important similarity. The career for the vast majority of the highly successful women and men in financial services is largely entrepreneurial. Therefore, it is not surprising that most of the financial services female professionals in this study who earn more than $500,000 per year own their own businesses. More than 65 percent of the women featured in this book and 60 percent of the most highly compensated women completing the WIFS survey are business owners. This means that they are the CEOs of their own companies, sign their own paychecks, and are responsible for the incomes of all of their employees (typically called team members by these women). Like the other business owners who are their clients, they must plan for the sale or succession of their businesses, fund their own retirements (and often the retirements of their employees), and pay for insurance for their families and most of their team members. Many also own or rent their own office space and pay many thousands of dollars each month in business expenses, everything from phone systems to computers to stationery. In addition, they contract with other professionals who advise them on aspects of running their business and/or work with their clients in areas where they do not have expertise.

## SUCCESSFUL WOMEN IN FINANCIAL SERVICES HAVE DIVERSE BUSINESS MODELS

Approximately half of the women featured in this book are financial representatives for insurance companies. Others are financial advisors working with various broker-dealers or are fee-based planners working in a business owned by themselves or another financial professional. A few are totally independent from any insurance company or broker-dealer.

Most of the women, no matter their relationship with a financial services company, describe themselves as entrepreneurs. Most do not earn a salary or receive a paycheck; instead, they work for commissions, overrides, fees, and percentages of assets under management (AUM). Their incomes are self-generated and variable. One woman, now a district manager for a major insurance company, frequently makes this tongue-in-cheek comment about her career, "Every morning, I get up without a job. I have to go out every day and find work."

## ADVANTAGES AND DISADVANTAGES OF AN ENTREPRENEURIAL CAREER

There are many advantages to an entrepreneurial career. Successful women in the financial services community cite independence, flexible schedules, high-income potential, working with successful people, and making a difference in the lives of individuals, families, and businesses as some of the major reasons why they love their careers.

At the same time, none of these successful women will say it was easy growing her business. Particularly in the early years, when the learning curve is steepest and the income the most variable, the job requires time, risk taking, willingness to fail and come back to work the next day, time management skills, interpersonal skills, belief in oneself, and a big dream. And the business does not blossom overnight or even in a few years. The incredibly successful women interviewed for this book have an average tenure in the career of twenty-five years. One of the youngest of the financial professionals has been in the career for eight years, the most experienced for forty-two years.

The work in the early stages of building the business is time-intensive and difficult. Over time, their work schedules become more flexible and they are able to spend more time out of the office. However, even as they have more time for themselves and their families, their responsibility to employees and clients increases and becomes more complex.

If you aspire to be a financial services professional, you should consider the many rewards you, your family, and your clients may reap. However, you must also recognize that you will be entering a field that requires a significant amount of knowledge and skill that you will need to gain within a relatively short period of time. And building the career you dream of is likely to take many years. This chapter will examine what the successful women who participated in this and other studies have said has been valuable to them as they have built their careers and businesses.

# WOMEN BEGINNING CAREERS IN FINANCIAL SERVICES NEED SUCCESSFUL FEMALE ROLE MODELS AND FEMALE-FRIENDLY MANAGERS

The critical importance of role models and mentors in the success of women in the financial services industry can be seen in an analysis of the data from the 2012 WIFS survey of women financial services professionals. When asked about their first jobs in the industry, greater than 35 percent of the women respondents who earn more than $500,000 per annum reported that they started their careers working with either a family member (21 percent) or a person they admired (15 percent). Whereas only 7.9 percent of women earning less than $200,000 per year began their careers working with a family member or a person they admired.[27] Although not surprising, the analysis of this data seems to confirm that women entering the financial services industry are not as likely to be successful if they do not have successful role models early in their careers.

By observing successful female role models in the profession, young female initiates can learn how women conduct themselves in the career and experience successful, female-initiated, woman-centered business models. This can provide these young women with the inspiration and vision they need for staying the course when they experience the inevitable bumps in the road of their new career.

The CFP Board of Standards Women's Initiative study (WIN) found that "the lack of female role models and networks for women can be seen as both a cause and effect of the low representation of women in financial planning."[28] The dearth of women currently in financial services, particularly in entrepreneurial careers, means that many young women entering the financial services industry begin their own careers with few or no female role models. Most of the respondents to the WIFS survey and the successful female professionals interviewed for this book point out that the industry continues to be a male-dominated profession with even fewer women in the managerial ranks of offices, agencies, and companies. Many of the women in this study with very long careers in the industry say that although there are more female recruits today than when they entered the business, there are no more women with five or more years experience in the business than twenty-five years ago.

Statistics provided by financial services companies seem to show that these women are correct.

The lack of women managers in financial services is, perhaps, an even larger problem than the small number of successful female role models if young women entering the industry are to become successful. According to the WIFS and WIN studies, young female financial services professionals need female role models and strong female advocates in order to advance in their careers.

The WIN study found that "women do not like to advocate for themselves."[29] Hence the lack of female role models and the small minority of female manager and advocates are two critical reasons why more women do not enter and remain in the industry. Without female role models, mentors, advocates, and managers, it is much more difficult for women to clearly identify a path to success. Also, the WIN survey suggests that women who enter the career and exit it early often leave because they do not have successful female role models. These young women need to see how successful women run their businesses. Many are uncomfortable running their businesses as they see male colleagues running theirs. And if these women entering the financial services profession have neither role models nor advocates, what they do have is a "chute" that can "slide [them] off a course that otherwise could lead to a career in financial planning."[30]

## PARENTS WHO ARE IN THE FINANCIAL SERVICES INDUSTRY ARE OFTEN EFFECTIVE ROLE MODELS

Of the twenty-three highly successful female financial services professionals featured in this book, four (more than 17 percent) started their careers with family members as role models. Two (Delynn Dolan Alexander and Melanie Shanty) came into the industry with mothers who were successful financial professionals. For Melanie and Delynn, their mothers remain their most important role models. Both Delynn and Melanie credit their mothers with much of their early and continued success.

Juli McNeely and Paula Zonin joined their fathers in the industry. Interestingly, Juli and Paula both indicate that although their fathers were positive role models, they did not do business in a way that was comfortable for their daughters. Juli says:

> My father's style was very different than mine, and he wasn't the best person for me to learn from ... Females learn and sell differently than men, and if you are taught a process that is not comfortable for you or you are not allowed to establish your own process, you will have a much harder time finding success.

Paula says this a little differently but comes to a similar conclusion:

> My mentor in my career was my father. He was a Berkshire Life general agent. I was trained with hard-core old school tactics. Basically, your day could not end until at least ten appointments were scheduled ... At the beginning of my career, I thought I was a failure.

So even though both women had positive parental role models as they began their careers, it was not their fathers' career maps or ways of doing business that they followed on their journeys in the business. Juli's and Paula's experiences learning the business from their fathers further supports the need for successful female role models for young women. Supportive—even loving—men may not be enough.

## MENTORS ARE ACTIVE PARTICIPANTS IN THE DEVELOPMENT OF THE NEW PROFESSIONAL

What is a mentor? Are mentors role models? Often mentors, particularly when sought, begin as role models. The key difference between being a role model and a mentor is participation. The role model may not even know that she is one. It is possible that she has never met the young female financial professional. However, the mentor is an active participant in the development of the young professional.

The mentor and the young professional (mentee) work together in developing the young woman's business. Both may benefit from this relationship, but the primary benefactor is the young professional mentee. Role models and mentors are important throughout a career and a life. It is not only those who are young in the business who benefit from finding a role model or working with a mentor. That is why true professionals continue to attend professional meetings to seek inspiration from others, join study groups to learn from peers, seek mentoring relationship, and hire coaches.

## CAN MANAGERS BE ROLE MODELS, MENTORS, AND ADVOCATES?

In the previous section of this chapter, we mentioned female managers must also serve as advocates for women in the profession. This begs the question: Is a female manager always a role model, a mentor, and an advocate? It is possible—but very difficult—to be all four. Management is very complex, and it may be even more difficult for female than male managers in the industry.

Where do female managers find their own successful female role models and mentors? Most managers cannot be everything to everyone at all times. Good managers, whether female or male, recognize this by setting policies and crafting environments that allow others to play the roles they cannot, when they cannot. Good managers establish and administer offices, agencies, and companies that are friendly for males and females and advocate equally for each gender. Good managers understand the needs of both the female and male recruits and attempt to develop policies and procedures that allow those of both genders to succeed.

If there are few female role models in the financial services profession, there are possibly even fewer female mentors. Why? A role model simply is—she need not be doing anything. However, in order to be a role model, she must be visible and not fly under the radar. She may speak at company or industry meetings, receive awards from her company and the industry, or publish or appear in articles in company or industry publications. However, being a mentor is much more difficult and results in less public recognition. A mentor is a teacher, a friend, a mother, and a cheerleader. A mentor may also be a role model. She must work at relationship if she is to help her young mentee succeed in the business. Although some companies and professional organizations, such as MDRT and WIFS, have formalized mentoring programs that attempt to successfully match a mentor with a mentee, many women seek mentors on their own.

## MANY WOMEN MUST SEEK AND FIND THEIR OWN FEMALE ROLE MODELS AND MENTORS

Since most of the successful female financial services professionals featured in this book did not have family members as role models, they either joined an office with a manager they respected or sought their own role models and mentors. As the first female recruited in an agency of twenty-five men, Robelynn Abadie was fortunate to have a supportive manager, but for her that was not enough. As previously discussed, because she was a single mom with two young children and a new business, she needed female role models and mentors who had succeeded in spite of the difficulties inherent in balancing motherhood and demanding careers. When she could not find these women locally, she persevered and eventually found two life-long mentors at the national meeting of WIFS (then WLUC).

## MALE ROLE MODELS AND MENTORS CAN FILL A VOID FOR MANY WOMEN

For many of the women interviewed for this book, their primary role models and mentors were men. There simply were not enough women in their offices or in the industry to easily find female role models or mentors. And like Robelynn, even if she found one or more female role models, the women might not be willing or able to give their time to mentor.

Lisa Sappenfield Boyer, like Robelynn Abadie, sought her own mentor. She met him at a school that was sponsored by her broker-dealer (Transamerica). He helped her set goals to qualify for the company's summer meeting. She did qualify, and at that meeting, he helped her figure out how to qualify for her first Transamerica Leaders Conference. Again, his advice made all the difference, and she did qualify. In April 2014, Lisa attended her twenty-fifth consecutive Leaders Conference.

Pamela Gilmour also found a role model, mentor, colleague, and center of influence all in one person. This man was not in her agency, but he was in the financial services industry. She says that he helped her build her business through example and partnership. He was the owner of a property and casualty office. "One of his unique services was that he would have a face-to-face annual review with all of his clients."

Every Tuesday he would schedule three or four of these meetings, and Pamela would go on the appointments with him. According to Pamela:

> He would introduce me to his clients as a financial planner and suggest that they meet with me. I would later call them and set up an appointment. I grew my business-owner clients by going on his appointments, and learned about his clients and his clients' businesses.

Pamela and the property and casualty agent partnered and shared commissions for the insurance business she placed. Since he was not equity licensed, they did not share investment income. However, she referred all her clients to him for their property and casualty needs. Through him, what she learned about working with clients, and his willingness to partner with her, Pamela found a role model and mentor who conducted his business in a way she was comfortable and with whom she did not need to compete.

## BE CAREFUL THAT WHAT YOU WISH FOR DOES NOT CHANGE WHO YOU ARE

As discussed earlier, Pamela Gilmour readily admits that male role models and mentors can be important to a woman's career, but she also reports that there can be danger in women becoming "one of the guys" in the office. And as in her case, the danger might be personal. Her "drive for success" (Pamela's words) might have been good for her career, but it was not good for her marriage. She was so focused on succeeding and out producing her male counterparts that she became a workaholic. Because of her career-oriented intensity and her inability to unwind, her marriage ended in divorce.

## AN ASIDE: "WOMEN DON'T NEED MORE ADVICE, MEN DO."

Joanne Lipman, a former deputy managing editor of the *Wall Street Journal* and former editor in chief of *Condé Nast Portfolio*, says that there has been a flood of books, articles, and conferences directed at teaching women how to succeed in business leadership. She says in a recent *Wall Street Journal* article, "I am convinced that women don't need more advice, men do."[31]

She qualifies this statement with the following:

> Now don't get me wrong. I love men. I've spent my career as a journalist at publications read primarily by men. All my mentors were men. And most professional men I've encountered truly believe they are unbiased.
>
> That said, they are often clueless about the myriad ways in which they misread women in the workplace every day. Not intentionally. But wow. They misunderstand us, they unwittingly belittle us, and they do something they think is nice that instead just makes us mad. And those are the good ones.

## IN SHORT, MEN COULD USE A CAREER GUIDE ABOUT WOMEN

Most of the women featured in this book have had male mentors, including their fathers. Like Joanne Lipman, the women in this study love and respect men. For many of the reasons Ms. Lipman cites, as well as simply needing advice about how to blend children and a demanding career, a male mentor was simply not adequate. These successful women needed female mentors to show them how to negotiate, as only a woman could, the worlds of work, entrepreneurship, children, and family.

## CAN WOMEN SUCCEED WITHOUT A MENTOR? HOW CAN WOMEN HELP OTHER WOMEN SUCCEED?

Some of the successful women interviewed for this study say they never had a mentor. All of those women agree that not having a mentor has been a disadvantage in their careers. Most believe they would have made progress more quickly and been happier in their work sooner if they had had a mentor, particularly a female mentor. Recognizing this unfulfilled need in their own careers, most are now serving as mentors for young women in their companies or through professional organizations.

Gail Linn's comments speak for many of them:

> Mentorship is very important to me. Since I never had a mentor in my early years, it is important for me to give back and help others. Therefore, I have become a mentor through both MDRT and WIFS. At WIFS, I am both a mentor and a mentee. Experiences that offer support like this are very important, particularly to women. For that reason, I make it a point to attend the WIFS annual conference to connect with other women in this business. MetLife also has an annual Women's Forum that I attend every year to meet with the top women at MetLife.

MetLife's Women's Forum provided Gail with the opportunity to become a part of MetLife Women's Leadership Circle and participate in a female study group that meets monthly, over the phone, to discuss business and personal challenges. These opportunities to meet and network with other women in the industry are what the CFP® WIN study referred to as female networks. And as their study showed, these can be as critical to a woman's success in the industry as successful female role models. Some of these female networks are initiated and sponsored by companies and professional organizations, while others are informally organized by the women themselves. (More of these informal female networks will be discussed in the study group section of this chapter.)

Juli McNeely (left) with her MDRT women's study group.

## ONE PIECE OF ADVICE MANAGERS NEED: WOMEN WILL NOT FAKE IT BEFORE THEY MAKE IT

One piece of advice managers in the financial services industry, particularly male managers, need about women is that they are unlikely to succeed if required to sell products or services before they feel 100 percent confident about those products and services. In recent years, many studies have been done of women consumers of financial services products and services. All come to the same conclusion: women want to understand what they are purchasing, they want to know about the skills of their advisor, and they will do independent research before making a purchase or selecting an advisor. So it should be of no surprise that women entering the financial services industry feel the same way. They want to know about the products they will be selling and the services they will be offering.

Many women featured in this book or responding to the 2012 WIFS survey of women financial services professionals commented that they were required by their managers to call on prospects to set appointments and sell products before they were confident in their own knowledge of the products and services they were offering. The mantra heard in many offices of "fake it before you make it" is an anomaly and offensive to most women. According to the CFP® WIN survey, a woman's desire for knowledge, coupled with her lack of adequate information about financial planning and what it takes to be successful in the industry is a recipe for dissatisfaction and an early exit from the career.

Sheryl Sandberg, in her best-selling book *Lean In: Women, Work, and the Will to Lead*, cites an internal study done by Hewlett-Packard. The study found that men would apply for a job when they considered themselves 60 percent qualified.[32] However, women would not apply until they felt 100 percent qualified. This holds true for women in the WIFS study as well. Women responding to the 2012 survey and in interviews for this book report that unless they had obtained knowledge about the business prior to entering it, they were uncomfortable introducing financial products and services to prospects. Since early and frequent sales are critical to initial success for most new initiates in the financial services industry, many women leave the career before they have the knowledge they need to build a successful practice simply because they do not believe they know enough about the products to sell them.

Dianna Parker (CFP®, National Resource, Director of Planning, Southern Regional Planning Group) is a successful financial consultant with Sagemark Consulting/Lincoln Financial Advisors and a national resource for other Lincoln Financial advisors on estate and business planning. She says that in her early years in the business, she had "trouble distinguishing between true planning and implementation. It took me a while to learn the vast and important difference between delivering a comprehensive plan and implementing life insurance or investments. Now, I simply can't bring myself to implement an insurance plan or an investment portfolio without having gone through the planning process." According to Dianna, her lack of knowledge of planning and the frustration she felt because of it could have caused her to quit or be less successful in the career.

Other women also want to know that their clients are pleased with the recommendations they have made and work they have done before they feel comfortable asking for a referral to a potential client. As Dianna says of her current firm, "Once a client has become a raving fan, we ask them to introduce us to other people who may need the type of work we do."

In the 2012 WIFS survey, 50 percent of the most highly compensated women ($1,000,000+ annual income) said they built their businesses primarily through referrals; networking was also cited by 25 percent of these women. When comparing the most highly compensated women's referral-based businesses with the businesses of less highly compensated women, the percentage of women responding that working with referrals is the primary way she built her business decreases with each level of compensation (16.9 percent of women earning less than $75,000 of annual income rely on referrals, and 27.6 percent of women earning between $200,000 and $499,999 cite referrals as the primary way their business was built.). There are two primary reasons why successful women are less likely to have a referral-based business:

- Most of the respondents at lower levels of compensation are newer to the business and less comfortable asking for referrals.
- The women who do not yet have clients who are raving fans are both reluctant to ask for—and less likely to receive—referrals.

Since women report that knowledge is the key to feeling comfortable setting appointments, making recommendations, and asking for referrals, gaining this knowledge is a prerequisite to a woman's success in the business. Why do so few women have this knowledge and possess this confidence?

- Most women enter the industry with little or no knowledge of finance.
- The learning curve in the financial services industry is steep. There is also a great deal to learn in a short period of time.
- Income is most often based on a formula requiring production and commission.
- Success in the industry is based on income earned.

These together can lead to the early departure from the industry for many women who have the potential for success. Management needs to find ways to educate women prior to requiring them to meet with prospects. If this problem can be solved, many more women will stay the course and succeed at high levels.

## GAINING THE NECESSARY CONFIDENCE AND GIVING ADVICE TO PROSPECTS AND CLIENTS

As Dianna Parker says:

> Persevere. This is not an easy business to learn, not an easy business to begin, not an easy business to build, and certainly it's still a man's world. But I believe that women have something very unique and special to offer in this profession, and I would love to see more women entering. I know women have a natural aversion to the business, even for those with the math, analytical, and/or sales skills, primarily because of the typical compensation structure. And the broker-dealers [and insurance companies] have a natural aversion to women simply because they are fishing in a pond where about 90 percent of the fish are male.

There is no doubt that taking Dianna's advice to persevere is important if women are to be as successful as the women featured in this book. However, for many young women, perseverance seems impossible when faced with the fear of not knowing enough to do what is in the best interest of the client and realizing that if she does not set appointments and sell products, she will have no income. However, if women recognize their uniqueness and what they can offer to a client, perhaps they can communicate their natural empathy and nurturing qualities to their future prospects in the early days of their business. Women can ask their managers and mentors to help them find appropriate language to use when making appointments to meet with prospects. Women can begin by listening to their prospects and completing basic financial fact-finders and then discussing these fact-finders with more experienced financial professionals. With the assistance of these more senior professionals, they can present financial solutions to their prospects and share the compensation with their newly found partners.

## HOW WOMEN DEAL WITH THE CONUNDRUM: LACK OF CONFIDENCE LEADS TO LACK OF INCOME

Several of these women had no choice but to succeed and simply had to find ways to do so. As single mothers with children, they had to overcome their fear and aversion and find ways to earn a living. However, it is also important to note that several of these single moms learned how to succeed through role models and education. Robelynn Abadie, for example, credits the course work she did early in her career while studying for an LUTCF (Life Underwriters Training Council Fellow) for helping her begin her business successfully. NAIFA says on its website about LUTCF courses and the designation:

> Successful insurance and financial services careers are deeply rooted in product knowledge and effective sales skills. The new NAIFA/LUTCF curriculum will combine product-focused education with hands-on sales training to help newer advisors thrive in a competitive industry.

Juli McNeely is the first female president of NAIFA:

> I first obtained the LUTCF designation early in my career. That proved extremely valuable for someone who didn't have a clue how to sell anything.

Gail Linn reiterates the importance of this educational program in her professional development:

> Not only did the LUTCF designation become my first achievement, but earning it taught me how to prospect and grow my business.

Some of the successful women in this study actually began their professional training and gained knowledge of the industry, products, and processes before working as personal producers or starting their own businesses. A few pursued undergraduate or graduate degrees in finance or business. Some, like Delynn Dolan Alexander, did college internships in financial services companies. However, academic training in the field was the exception rather than the rule. Young women today can actually pursue college programs in which they can earn the CFP® as a part of their coursework. If these programs are not available on their campuses, they can seek out local LUTCF, CFP®, or CLU (Chartered Life Underwriter) programs offered by professional organization or financial services companies in their communities. Most will welcome their involvement.

A larger number of the women in this study learned about the career in paying positions in insurance or financial planning offices, agencies, companies, or corporations prior to starting their own businesses. Betty Harris Custer, for example, worked her way through college as a clerk in an insurance office. After graduation, she became the office manager. Nancy Wolfe-Smith spent twelve of the first sixteen years of her career working in corporate leadership for State Farm (four as a supervisor in a corporate department and eight as a trainer of new agents). Toni Espey was a fire claim representative for State Farm and spent a year, while working for State Farm, interviewing with the man who was her first manager when she became a State Farm agent. Juli McNeely learned about finance while working in the banking industry prior to joining her father in his financial planning firm.

Robelynn Abadie sold cancer policies when she started her career. Melanie Shanty, today a financial advisor with Lincoln Financial, sold 403B nonprofit employees' retirement plans early in her career. Robelynn and Melanie earned their stripes by specializing in a single product (cancer policies) or market (employee benefits) prior to expanding their businesses into more comprehensive planning.

Pamela Gilmour started in product sales prior to entering the financial services industry. She reports that in an exit interview from her previous employer, the woman interviewing her asked what she would be earning in her new job.

Pamela answered, "There is no salary, and I don't know, but it's unlimited!"

The woman then asked her about what kind of benefits she would be getting.

Pamela replied, "None ... I have to get and pay for them myself."

The woman then said, "Do you know what you are doing?"

Pamela reports that the woman who interviewed her "was one of the first people to come in and work with me [as a financial advisor]. She continues to be one of my biggest cheerleaders."

## PROFESSIONAL DESIGNATIONS ARE IMPORTANT TO SUCCESSFUL WOMEN

The twenty-three women featured in this book hold an average of 2.2 professional designations each. Five hold three designations, two hold four, and three hold five. Even the two women who hold no designations talk about the importance of continuing to learn. One even suggests that she possibly could have been more successful if she had earned a CFP®, but she simply could not fit it in while raising children and building a business. The other has a CFP® on retainer to work with her clients as needed.

In the 2012 WIFS survey, 77.5 percent of women earning $500,000 to more than $1,000,000 per year held at least one designation; most held more than one. Nine of the successful women in this book hold the CFP® (Certified Financial Planner) designation. Most of these women refer to themselves as financial planners or wealth managers. Six of the women have earned both CLU (Chartered Life Underwriter) and ChFC (Chartered Financial Consultant) designations.

Most of these women began their careers in the insurance industry, although several have now become financial advisors and wealth managers. One of these women, Pamela Gilmour, began her career in the insurance industry and holds a CFP® and is also a CPA (Certified Public Accountant). One woman with a CFP® also has a ChFC (Chartered Financial Consultant) designation. Another with a CFP® has a CLU. All of these designations are rigorous. They require many courses and exams.

There are other designations held by these women. Most of the other designations held by these women provide them with specialty knowledge or skills, such as long-term care planning: CLTC and CASL. (See appendix D for the designations, organizations sponsoring or offering them, and website addresses.)

These women hold professional designations primarily because of the knowledge they gain through the courses they take to earn them. However, they also complete the coursework because what they learn helps them build personal confidence in the advice they give their clients. In addition, these designations show their prospects and clients, particularly those who research the qualifications of an advisor, that these women are qualified to provide them with financial advice.

The designations make their clients feel more confident in the abilities of their advisors. Designation, many of these women say, "Set me apart from others who do not have them." Many of the women in this study strongly believe that even with all of their education, knowledge, skills, and experience, they cannot do everything their clients need. They often work with specialists who can assist their clients in areas where the primary advisor does not have the expertise. If the women work independently or within a small group of advisors, they forge strategic professional relationships with other professionals, including attorneys, accountants, and various financial planning specialists. These relationships allow them to provide what their clients need without the primary financial advisor having to do so all by herself.

## LEARNING NEVER ENDS

One thing that all the women featured in this book agree upon is that learning never ends. In fact, Karen DeRose (CFP®, CRPC®, managing partner of DeRose Financial Planning Group, Lincoln Financial Advisors) says that, "Continuous learning and personal growth is one of eight core values of her company. Our education doesn't end with degrees, credentials and certifications—that's where it begins." These women also continue to read and study, often on their own, throughout their careers. They read professional journals regularly and books, both inspirational and professional, as often as possible. Cassettes, in earlier years, and CDs and downloads, today, allow them to listen to presentations they missed at company or organizational meetings.

All of the women featured in this book pursue education outside of their companies, but they also take advantage of all the training, education, and networking opportunities provided by their companies. In spite of the fact that the WIN survey finds that women (44 percent) are less likely to be pleased with their company's training programs than men (67 percent), the successful women featured in this study are not the women who give every possible excuse to *not* attend company training schools and events. These women take every opportunity to broaden their educations and network with colleagues. In fact, many of these women volunteer to participate in company programs that are not mandatory.

Most of the women featured in this book recognize that learning through teaching is a very good way to give back to the industry and increase the depth of their knowledge. Almost all the women mentor younger financial services professionals, and two hold the Certified Trainer designation. Dianna Parker works as an advisor in the area of estate planning for other Lincoln Financial advisors who do not have her depth of knowledge in this specialty.

Dianna Parker and her colleagues on the Lincoln's
Premier Partner Advisory Council (PPAC).

The bottom line for all of these women is taking advantage of all opportunities to learn. Learn as many things as possible as quickly as possible. If you cannot afford to persevere in the business for several years with very limited income while you learn what you need to be successful, consider taking a paying job in a financial services firm and studying and learning while on that job. When you are knowledgeable and confident, start your own business.

## COACHING CAN BE VERY IMPORTANT IN BUILDING A SUCCESSFUL BUSINESS

Education, training, and designations may not be enough for these successful women to be as knowledgeable and professional as possible. Even as mature, experienced financial services professionals, most of these women admit that they still need help and advice in many areas of their businesses. Because they know that it takes a village to run a business, they also have professional coaches. And many of these coaches work with the female financial professional, the business owner, and her team members.

The women say that they most often need a coach to help them to set and implement strategies and procedures for managing their businesses. Physicians and lawyers frequently have limited or no business acumen and hire business managers to help them run their businesses. Financial services professionals may be able to tell their clients how to protect their business risks or transition their businesses to new owners or family members, but they often need help running their own businesses. They have questions such as:

- When do I hire staff or team members?
- When and how do I let a staff person or team member go?
- How do I organize my staff or team for maximum efficiency?
- How do I make the most of my time?
- How do I organize my office so that it is client-centered and friendly?

Many of the successful women in this book comment that working with a coach has been very beneficial to the success of their businesses. According to Colleen Bowler:

> The best thing I did for my career was become a part of Strategic Coach®, an organization that works with entrepreneurs to help them increase their income and free time. It made such an impact [on me] that I am a part-time coach for them now.

These women believe that in order to be successful they need to invest in themselves and invest in their businesses, and there may be no better way to do that than to hire a coach. Several of the women have hired different coaches at different times in their careers based on what they are trying to achieve at that moment. Some want coaches who know the financial services business inside out who can help them determine and achieve a new level of production or improve their prospecting to more affluent clients. As one woman said in an anecdotal comment on the 2012 WIFS survey:

> When I started in this business, I met with anyone, no matter whether they had any money or not. I soon learned that, no matter how much I liked them, if they couldn't purchase products from me, I would soon starve. So, I had to find a way to meet more prosperous prospects who were just as likeable. I hired a coach to help me make the transition.

Some women also work with specialty coaches who help them do such things as deal with marketing, promotion, or technology. They ask the coach the following:

- How do I position myself so that when someone researches me via the Internet, they come away with an accurate and a positive impression of who I am and how I do my business?
- How do I overcome negativism that might appear in social media?

- How do I use social media in a way that can help me grow my business and still be compliant?
- How and where do I advertise?
- What things do I e-mail to clients and prospects and how often?
- What is the best "phone language" for my voice mail and for my staff to use when answering the phone?

The lists of questions highly successful women financial services business owners ask a coach are endless and change throughout their careers.

For the successful women who have hired coaches, they have made an investment in their businesses: personal and financial. Good business coaches are not inexpensive, and they shouldn't they be. Coaching and being coachable is also time-intensive. Although many new female financial services professionals may have the time, need a coach, and want a coach, they cannot afford to pay a coach.

What can young female professionals do to obtain the expertise a coach can provide without the resources to pay the full stipend of the coach?

- The first step might be checking with her company to see what kind of coaching opportunities might exist that are either free or inexpensive. Often, these are group phone coaching sessions. They may also be focused on a particular goal or expectation of the company, agency, or office. Even if the opportunities are free, there is a cost, and that is time. Young professionals, just as their more senior and successful colleagues, must do a cost-benefit analysis.
  - Am I getting what I need from these coaching sessions?
  - Do I come away from them with new goals and energy?
  - Do I feel more positive or negative about my business and myself after these sessions?
  - Are the sessions worth the time I am investing?
- The young female professional can also check with other young female professionals to determine if one or more of them might be interested in hiring a coach to do group sessions with them. Many study groups use coaches in this manner.

- Another option for young female professionals is to check organization websites (WIFS, MDRT, NAIFA, etc.) to find the names of coaches who give discounts to members of these organizations.
- She may also be able to contact a coach through the coach's website and ask if there is a group, non-company-specific coaching opportunity in which she could participate.
- If the young professional is a member of a study group (see next section), the study group might be able to negotiate with a coach to work with the entire group. Since most coaching is done over the phone, several study group members can participate in a single session. This can divide the cost of the coach between the members of the group.

## STUDY GROUPS CAN BE HELPFUL AT ANY STAGE OF A CAREER

What is a study group? A study group in the financial services industry is usually a group of professionals with similar interests or needs. The group might be very selective and include only top producers. To join the group, an invitation could be required. Some study groups, like the one Barbara Brazda Dietze belongs to, allow members to share goals and hold each other accountable for those goals. Some study groups focus on particular products or planning techniques.

In the anecdotal comments in the survey, one successful female services professional talked about a study group that she has been a member of for fifteen years. The group is called the Salty Dogs (based on the name of the restaurant where they first met). However, the name of the group is also appropriate because initially the membership, mostly female, concentrated on long-term care insurance and long-term care planning. The group now has more male than female members, meets face-to-face twice a year, has acquired many new members and lost mature members over the years, and now has the broader focus of retirement, health care, and estate planning. Most study groups keep their memberships to only a few professionals, but some can be as large as several hundred members.

There are many kinds of study groups:

- A study group can also have self-selected or appointed members who meet, not to talk about a specific topic, but rather to discuss personal as well as professional concerns. These groups can be long-lived, lasting over the professional lives of the members. Or the group might dissolve as members leave the business or decide the group no longer meets their needs.
- Groups can also be formed to address short-term concerns.
- Some study groups select and invite new members based on specific study-group-developed-requirements.
- Study groups might have members from different professions, for example: one member who represents financial services, another who represents law, another who represents accountancy, etc. These groups are designed to share ideas and clients. They are typically local.
- Study groups frequently are made up of professionals who all are affiliated with a single company.
- Study groups also may have members across companies. Frequently these multi-company study groups are formed through associations made at professional organization meetings.
- Professional organizations and companies might facilitate the formation of study groups.

Many financial services professionals belong to more than one study group. The key to the success of a professional study group is that the study group

- meets the needs of its members;
- is content-centered;
- has rules about attendance and participation;
- has active participants; and
- meets regularly.

Many groups meet face-to-face one or two times a year, but they may meet over the phone more frequently. Some groups have an off-site meeting at a resort once a year that includes spouses and partners of members.

All group members must be comfortable with the financial obligations of the group.

Robelynn Abadie (right) with her study group in Mexico, 1983.

Many of the successful female financial services professionals featured in this book belong to study groups of various types. Because of the success of these women, as measured by their companies, a large percentage of them regularly qualify and attend the leaders' meetings and events of their companies. Of course, these study groups differ from those above in that the membership varies each year, is determined by goals set by the company, and is primarily based on production. They also differ in that the company typically sets the agenda for the meeting, although the qualifiers or a leadership group of the qualifiers may have influence over the agenda.

Also a large number of these women participate in professional organization study groups based, at least in part, on their financial success in the business. Sometimes these groups relate to a specific concern of the organization, such as the Women's Initiative (WIN) of CFP®. At other times, the group is made up of members who simply qualify based on production. Probably the most widely cited of these groups in the financial services industry is MDRT's Top of the Table (TOT), requiring approximately $1 million of annual production as measured by the companies that participate in MDRT. Although some qualifiers may serve on committees who set the agenda and invite speakers, the leadership of the organization does most of this.

Several of the women in this study have been founding members or leaders of WIFS local chapters in their communities or companies. These local chapters often become study groups for many of their members. Lisa Sappenfield Boyer, for example, has been a leader of WIFS, not in her local community, but with her broker-dealer, Transamerica. In 2009, Pamela Gilmour founded her WIFS local chapter, which now has forty-five members. Although not official study groups, these chapters serve the same purpose for many women and can be joined by any female (some chapters even have male members) financial services professional.

## SUCCESSFUL WOMEN BELONG TO—AND ARE ACTIVE IN— PROFESSIONAL ORGANIZATIONS

Every female successful financial services professional featured in this book belongs to—and is active in—one or more professional organizations. Some, like Robelynn Abadie and Pamela Gilmour, were founding members of professional organizations. Many, like Juli McNeely (2014 president of NAIFA), Kathleen Godfrey (2010 president of WIFS), and Robelynn Abadie (2002 president of WIFS, president of the MDRT Foundation, and president of Association of Health Insurance Advisors) have served in major national and international leadership positions.

Women leaders of major professional organizations: Susan Combs, president WIFS, Daralee Barbera, president of GAMA (General Agents and Manager Association), and Juli McNeely, president of NAIFA.

All of these women learned early in their careers how important these organizations were—and are—to their professional development. For many of them, the organizations provided the role models and mentors they did not find in their own agencies, offices, and companies (MDRT and WIFS). For others, these organizations gave them the initial education they so desperately needed in order to feel confident enough to get started in the business (NAIFA and LUTCF). At the meetings of these professional organizations—and the speakers they listened to—many of these successful women were inspired to keep moving forward and stay focused on their goals even when everything seemed to be pulling them toward the revolving door.

As their careers progressed and their businesses grew, these women made contact through these professional organizations with other like-minded successful professionals. These women often provided them with friendship and insight. For many, these organizations put the successful women in touch with some of the most successful people, women and men, in the business. All the women in this study recognize that a large reason for their success is that they surround themselves with positive, successful people.

These organizations often provided female-centered study groups and recognition. Sometimes this recognition was obtained from the leadership the women provided to the organization (rather than production). At other times, it was through speaking or membership in top-producer groups. And more importantly, for most of these women, these top-producer groups introduced them to other successful financial services professionals from around the country and the world. The successful professionals—the women would have never met in any other way—have provided transcendent moments that moved their careers to new levels.

≈

## SUCCESSFUL WOMEN ACCEPT THE CHALLENGE TO GROW WHEN THE TIME IS RIGHT

Several years ago, Jennifer Borislow (the second female and 2012 president of MDRT) spoke at a WIFS annual conference in Boston. She talked of her business model, which had primarily provided benefits for administrators, board members, and employees at private schools in New England. Jennifer had built a remarkable reputation and phenomenally successful business working with these schools.

At an MDRT Top of the Table meeting, one of her fellow qualifiers challenged her to grow her business in a new direction. He pointed out to her that among her group of benefits clients she had a pool of people who trusted her and needed her advice with sophisticated individual financial planning issues. At that time, she wasn't interested in pursuing a new line of business, was happy with her current business model, and was proud of how successful she had become. However, she continued to think about his challenge.

Later, she began looking for a business partner she could trust with whom to pursue this line of business with her valued clients. She found him, but it took two years for her to convince him to join her. Now she and her business partner are more successful than they could have been without each other.

Jennifer's story is not unique. Many significant producers have been challenged by other equally successful members of professional organizations and study groups (or sometimes their coaches) to move their business to the next level. If they were not actively involved in these organizations, the women may not have been inspired to focus on their goals—and the challenges may never have been made. These challenges, from like-minded professionals they respect, were the "transcendent moments" that helped build the female financial professional's business beyond her dreams.

All of the women featured in this study have moved their businesses to the next level several times during their careers. They have, at times, taken professional leaves of absence from their journeys to the top of the profession. Children and care of other family members are the most common reasons for the interludes. However, after their care and nurturing services are no longer necessary, or at least not critically needed, they did one or more of the following:

- created a new business plan
- sought inspiration from a professional organization and meetings
- talked to colleagues who had made similar quantum leaps
- sought a new mentor and mentored a new colleague
- read and studied professional books
- worked toward a new designation
- hired a new coach
- joined a new study group
- found a new business partner with skills that were needed to grow the practice
- hired new team members or staff (sometimes this required letting go of team members or staff who did not fit into the new plan or could not contribute to the goals)
- shared her new plan with her clients, asked their advice and help, and gained new referrals
- found new, independent office space

# CHAPTER 6 ——————————————————————
# BUSINESS MODELS AND PLANS

**Marketing Mission**

We forge mutually beneficial relationships with our clients, empowering them to become the financial architects of their own futures through our *strategic planning process*, based upon our core values approach to planning "Life happens ... plan for it!"

—Karen DeRose, CFP®, CRCP®, Managing Partner, DeRose Financial Planning Group, Lincoln Financial Advisors

## DIVERSE BUSINESS PLANS LEAD TO SUCCESS

The diversity of the business plans of the twenty-three very successful financial services professionals featured in this book may seem somewhat surprising on the surface. There was a time not long ago when insurance agents sold insurance, banks took deposits and administered loans, and securities brokers sold investments. Until the 1999 repeal of the Glass-Steagall Act (passed by Congress in 1933 to separate commercial and investment banking), the financial services industry was largely compartmentalized. De-compartmentalizing the financial services industry began in the 1980s and was completed when Glass-Steagall was repealed during the Clinton administration.

# CHANGES IN THE INDUSTRY IMPACT THE BUSINESS MODELS OF SUCCESSFUL WOMEN

Today, financial planners can specialize in a single insurance product or can run a comprehensive planning business for which they receive fees, commissions, and income from assets under management (AUM). The businesses of these women range from one insurance agent who specializes in life insurance with no employees to an agent and owner of two offices selling ninety-six different products and services with eighteen employees in a variety of roles.

Some of the women in this study are primarily in the insurance business, others focus almost exclusively on equities and investments, and some are fee-based financial planners who provide a full range of financial services to their clients. Two of the women in the study design benefits for business owners, executives, and employees. One woman makes most of her income from property and casualty (P and C) insurance products, although she and her employees sell about sixty different products.

One of the women owns an independent SEC-regulated Registered Investment Advisory firm. Another is a regional director of planning and a national resource on estate and business planning for a large insurance, financial planning, and investment company. She serves as a resource for financial planners around the country, and she works directly with their clients. One of the women she frequently partners with is also featured in this study and is the sole proprietor for a fee-based planning firm that sells investments and insurance products.

Other women in the study are managing partners or registered principals of their own firms, some of which are incorporated. Several of the women have "doing business as" (DBA) identities approved by the insurance companies with whom they are affiliated. These women often do the full range of insurance, investment, and planning options of their counterparts who work in or with financial planning corporations.

It is important to note that one woman (Monica Jones) featured in this book, who entered the business following a long career as a teacher, is employed by a company whose primary business is not insurance. Every year for Monica is a new year. She receives no renewals, streams, or overrides for previous insurance products she has sold. She says that her organizational skills have allowed her to experience rapid success. She has taken to heart what she has learned from other women in the industry. Through her affiliation with Women in Insurance and Financial Services (WIFS), she has learned the importance of continuous contact with clients. Even though she is not compensated for working with clients to whom she has previously sold products, she recognizes the importance of keeping in contact with them. After all, the term life insurance policy the client bought from her when she or he was young may not be the most appropriate product when the children are grown and the client is more affluent.

As mentioned in her profile in chapter one, Monica keeps in touch with her clients by sending them personal handwritten notes. This takes her a lot of time, but it is time worth spending. Not only does it make her clients feel that she cares about them but it also keeps the concept of protecting their families in the forefront of their planning. Consequently, many of her previous clients become continuous clients as they solve the risk needs of their families and businesses. Since they are satisfied clients, they refer new clients to her.

Today, there are almost unlimited possibilities under the financial services umbrella for intelligent, ambitious, and highly principled women and men. What a woman decides to pursue depends on many things, including personal experience, education, age, marital status, motherhood, prior career experience, financial stability, interests, and opportunities. However, there are common core elements found in the business plans of each of the twenty-three very successful financial services professionals featured in this study. They include the following:

- Each of these financial services professionals has a plan and can articulate her plan.
- All of their business plans are based on the core value of *the client comes first*.
- Each of these women is passionate about what she does to help her clients succeed.
- If the woman has employees, and most do, she considers them to be members of her team, empowers them to succeed, holds them accountable for the work they do, and rewards their success.

- *Giving back* is a core value of each of the plans.
- Each plan is based on the woman's own definition of success.

## A WOMAN'S EVOLVING DEFINITION OF SUCCESS AFFECTS HER BUSINESS PLAN

Although most women earning more than $500,000 per annum who participated in 2012 WIFS survey entered the financial services industry prior to age thirty, many did not, including several featured in this book. Obviously, the longer she is in the business, the more time she has to build her business—and the greater the likelihood she will achieve financial success. This is particularly true in financial services since so much of a producer's income is based on past business, and most new clients are referrals from satisfied clients. Financial services is a business that builds upon itself. Spending more hours per day at the business may or may not lead to greater income, but spending more years in the business virtually always does. Therefore, young women who join the industry immediately after finishing their education are more likely than older women who join the industry after another career to define their success based on higher levels of production or assets under management. However, even though the women may define success based on production goals, they typically do not articulate these production goals in their business plans.

The financial services industry often attracts career changers, particularly women. With the right set of circumstances, it can provide the flexibility to have and raise children while one continues to work. Nearly half of the women featured in this book already had children when they entered the profession; nineteen of the twenty-three women in the study now have children. Having children, particularly as a single parent, may mean that she might choose or be compelled to devote more time to her children than to her job. Some of these women actually worked part-time for a number of years. Others left their own businesses and took salaried jobs in the industry for part of their careers, returning to their own businesses when their children were more independent.

A woman's responsibility to her children may be why the vast majority of women featured in this book did not tie their success to their current income. In fact, none of the women participating in the in-depth interviews for this book mentioned her current income as a measure of her success, in spite of the fact that her company and the industry always use income as the primary measure of success. Women with children may grow their businesses with stops and starts and are likely to define success differently at various stages of their lives. While adding twenty or more new clients every year may be an important goal when the woman can devote full-time to her business, she may be forced to focus only on current clients in the years when she has young children at home. Women's business goals and business plans are likely to change many times during their careers rather than remaining on a steady path forward.

Many variables affect how women financial services professionals judge their personal and professional success. Since all of their business plans have clear goals that the women expect to achieve, these goals as they relate to business growth vary widely. With the exception of one woman who sent us slides she used in a company presentation, none of the women used income, assets under management (AUM), or any other remunerative measure as goals in their business plans. All of them, like Karen DeRose in the articulation of her company's marketing mission above, had client-centered missions, goals, and core values. Likewise, it was not unusual for the women to have personal objectives, such as number of workdays per week or amount of time spent with family, included in their business plans. The vast majority of women also articulated goals for their team members. Community and industry service goals, personal and team educational goals, and family goals were also included in many of the women's business plans.

## EACH SUCCESSFUL WOMAN HAS A UNIQUE BUSINESS PLAN, BUT ALL HAVE COMMON CORE VALUES

In this section, we will look at the business plans of some of the women featured in the book. The primary core value of each of these women's business plans is that she focuses on the client first. We will start with the most comprehensive business plan submitted by these women.

## KAREN DEROSE'S CLIENT-CENTERED BUSINESS PLAN

Karen DeRose (center) and her team.

Karen DeRose entered the financial services profession eighteen years ago when she was thirty-four years old and had two children, ages twelve and five. Today she is the managing partner of DeRose Financial Planning Group. Her son Anthony (MBA, CPA, JD) is now an associate planner in her firm. They have three salaried full-time employees and two part-time assistants. Their goal is to grow the firm to three planners by 2016. This will allow them to double their revenue and nearly double the value of the practice, something that is very important in multigenerational businesses.

The marketing mission of the DeRose Financial Planning Group appears in the box at the beginning of the chapter and articulates the client-centered approach of the practice.

To get a flavor of the client-centered language used in Karen's business plan, read some of the DeRose Financial Planning Groups' objectives and core values below:

- Focus our efforts on building a positive *client experience* through touch points and services, taking direction from our clients (based on a client survey conducted in October 2013).
- Monthly *reach out* to clients on old *life* policies to ensure they are still appropriate based on clients' needs and cost effectiveness ... Take advantage of conversions for clients who may now be uninsurable.
- The associate planner will help build on existing client relationships and attend all client meetings.
- When discussing existing insurance policies, the following language is used: "to ensure that we are not only building their wealth but protecting their wealth."
- A practice welcome kit will be used to brand, communicate, and systematize the nature of the practice's relationship with clients.
- [When discussing new software to be used by staff:] This should free up staff time and have them focus on promoting the client experience with world-class service by being proactive.
- [From executive summary:] The first portion of the marketing plan speaks specifically to creating a well thought-out client experience with critical leverage points necessary in staying in constant contact with current clients.
- 75 percent of the practice's new clients come from our satisfied clients.
- Our mission: To better serve our clients in the Chicagoland area through passion and integrity by providing holistic, practical financial planning advice along with experienced investment management that empowers our clients to reach their personal and financial aspirations.

Karen DeRose's business plan does not leave out the importance of a work environment that promotes a better life for all team members. Below are three of their core values:

- *Teamwork:* As a work family, we will look out for one another and help each other whenever possible.

- *Have fun:* Just because it is work does not mean we should not enjoy working with one another.
- *Balanced life:* We will continue to realize the importance of our family and friends—and never allow our work to neglect them.

Another very interesting aspect of DeRose Financial Planning Group's business plan is the emphasis on branding, technology, public relations, and social media. Use of these technologies is also client-focused in the DeRose plan. Here are a few items from the plan:

- Implement *Redtail CRM* software. Be a user of this software and also *mine* business by reaching out to clients with life events, contribution reminders, and other relevant planning opportunities that affect them personally.
- Develop a PR campaign to be acknowledged as the *premier financial planning group* with our unique planning process and client experience.
- Continue to promote our *E-Worth* manager.
- Promote our new website.
- Create referral process *touch points.*
- Send contribution [to retirement plans] e-mail reminders.
- From the executive summary: *Touchpoint* system of at least twenty touches annually through Monthly *Wealthlink* E-Newsletters, Annual Thanksgiving Wine gift, holiday card, etc.
- Social media and online presence continues to be at the forefront. Take the time to research and develop an important strategy that is FINRA compliant and takes advantage of this *wave*. Be at the forefront of promoting our practice online and reaching the next generation of successful clients.

Also, the plan focuses on the importance of developing new relationships and continuing old relationships:

- Focus on three networking groups this year ... with the intent of building trusted relationships for referring business.

- Associate planner in 2014 will maintain his informal Chicago network group but also find a network group already in existence that promotes business.
- Deepen our trusted advisor relationships.

Client-centered goals, objectives, and practices are central to the business plans of successful women. Similar themes and client-centered language appear in the business plans of the other successful female financial services professionals.

DeLynn Dolan Alexander and Reena Bland (Alexander Financial Services, Northwestern Mutual) use this client-centered language in their plan:

> We do comprehensive financial planning, both fee based and non–fee based, with individuals who are business owners or executives of businesses. Our planning process clarifies our clients' goals and objectives for their financial future, including planning for retirement, education, legacy, and philanthropy. Our analytics team assesses their insurance, investments, wills, trusts, and other assets in collaboration with a client's legal and tax advisors. We advise our clients on their efficiencies to make these goals a reality.

Lisa Sappenfield Boyer (CFP®, Registered Principal, Investment Advisor Representative, Transamerica) also has a son who joined her in the business right after he graduated from college. Her mission is: *To help people who care about their family and others live the life they want to live and become financially independent.* To achieve this client-centered mission, she has a customer-service employee who has been with her for fourteen years and a financial assistant who prepares weekly client reviews and does research. In addition to these two, she has a part-time employee who helps with paperwork and projects. Lisa says of her business:

> My practice revolves around our personalized reviews that are spread out weekly throughout the year. I do

reviews, allocate portfolios, finalize plans, and decide on distributions ... Everything else is delegated to the appropriate employee. I also manage the business and financial side of the practice.

Colleen Bowler (CFP®, Lincoln Financial/Strategic Wealth Partners) describes her practice as "independent under Lincoln Financial's umbrella." Although she has her own employees and pays rent, salaries, and expenses, like other independent entrepreneurs, she also has "the backing and usage of a very large planning organization through Lincoln. My team and I use their expertise regularly and pay them to input and put together our plans, allowing us to do what we do best—take care of our clients."

Barbara Brazda Dietze (CLU, ChFC, Financial Adviser, Eagle Strategies Group LLC, New York Life) focuses her business on insurance, estate, and financial planning. She works with several advisors who "lend specialty to my practice." Also she has seven planning associates "who orchestrate custom business, estate, retirement, education, and financial planning models for clients." Barbara also has a twenty-three-year-old son who has started a career in the financial services industry and may one day join her in the business.

Kathleen Godfrey (Registered Investment Advisor, Godfrey Financial Associates) is the only totally independent financial planner among the twenty-three women featured in this book. Because Kathleen is totally independent, she has worked hard to develop trusted relationships and contracts with other advisors: the CFP® she has on retainer, the estate attorney, and the property and casualty insurance professional she has contracted to assist her clients in areas where she lacks expertise. A video on Kathleen's website addresses the client experience in her practice: *Let us design your personal financial roadmap.* Her website emphasizes her independence, unbiased advice, and integrity.

Toni Espey (CASL, Antonia C. Epsey Insurance Agency, Inc., State Farm) has a positioning statement for her agency and herself. It reflects the client-centered approach she and her team employ.

Toni Espey runs a successful State Farm Agency in Coconut Creek, Florida. She works with individuals and families in the community who want to manage the risks of everyday life, recover from the unexpected, and realize their dreams. Toni helps people realign their insurance and financial portfolios by giving honest feedback. As an accomplished professional with twenty-seven years of experience, Toni has helped empower hundreds of policyholders.

Nancy Wolfe-Smith (CLU, FLMI, LUTCF, MBA, Nancy Wolfe-Smith Insurance Agency, Inc., State Farm) says of her agency's vision:

Our vision is to help our clients take care of their families. We truly care about them and their needs, so we strive to be their future managers, helping to give them hope. Our goal is to help all of our clients reach their American Dream. Our mission statement is simple and follows our vision: Protecting what you love is not just important to us; it's the right thing to do for you and your family!

Robelynn Abadie (CAP®, RFC, LUTCF, CHRS®, CSA, Founder and CEO, Abadie Financial Services), like many of the successful women featured in this book, is constantly thinking of the next steps for her business. This was not a luxury she had in the earliest days of her practice when she was a single mother and needed to focus on a business model that would allow her to work only during the days when her children were at school. Today, she works primarily in the benefits marketplace, a business she established because business owners and executives wanted to meet with her during regular work hours. She says of her current business model:

My business is highly concentrated in corporate and employee benefits, implementation of ACA (Affordable

Care Act) and continuing education to do that effectively. [This] has taken most of my time the past couple of years.

However, Robelynn has been thinking about and planning her next steps. She plans to sell the benefits portion of her business in the next three to five years so that she can concentrate on her passion and work with clients of like mind: charitable giving through estate planning and life insurance. She has prepared for this by recently earning a new designation (CAP®, Chartered Advisor in Philanthropy) and joining a study group of charitably minded philanthropists from various professions and businesses.

## A CLIENT-CENTERED TEAM IS CRUCIAL TO THE SUCCESS OF WOMEN'S BUSINESS PLANS

Putting together the appropriate team to work with clients sometimes involves keeping your eyes and your mind open. However, developing a team of professionals who work well together with clients toward common goals is critical to the success of these women.

To Nancy Wolfe-Smith, her team's interaction with the clients is of utmost importance:

> My team members and I are dedicated to positive, ethical, and caring interaction with our clients and each other. We are committed to building our knowledge base, taking on new challenges with optimism, and growing the business. We meet daily, weekly, monthly, and quarterly to ensure that we are working together toward the same goal. We work as one to help our clients.

Delynn Dolan Alexander's partnership and friendship with Reena Bland occurred during a difficult time in Delynn's professional life and has been critical to the success of their business and quality of their team. When Delynn recognized that her dream of becoming a managing partner was not going to occur, Reena was a five-year financial representative and field director working in Delynn's agency.

Delynn and Reena were both single and would get together after work, often over a beer, to discuss their dreams and goals. It soon became clear to Delynn that Reena was the kind of person she would like to work with for the rest of her career. Together, they planned the next step. They would become equal business partners and open a financial services practice that would meet all the financial needs of their clients. Today, Delynn is the chief business development officer, and Reena is the chief financial officer of Alexander Financial Services, one of the most successful full-service practices in their company. They have built a team of client-centered professionals, allowing each of them to do what she or he does best and to provide all of the financial services their clients need.

## THE JOB TITLES OF THESE SUCCESSFUL WOMEN TELL US ABOUT THEIR BUSINESS MODELS

The successful women featured in this book were not asked in the in-depth interviews to describe in a few words their current job, position, or title in the industry. However, most of them provided this information through their business plans, the designations they have earned, and their websites. Fifteen of the twenty-three women (65 percent) interviewed for this book call themselves one of the following: wealth manager, financial planner, or financial advisor. In other words, most of these successful women interviewed for this book do *holistic financial planning* for their clients.

The high percentage of highly successful women who do comprehensive or holistic planning as their primary business model also was evident in the data of the 2012 WIFS survey. Of the women who completed that survey and earned more than $500,000 per year, over 60 percent reported that their current job in the industry was financial advisor, wealth manager, or business owner. Since most of the women featured in this book could also describe themselves as a business owner, the percentages appear to be congruent between the most successful women responding to the survey and those participating in the in-depth interviews.

The 2012 WIFS survey shows that women at income levels below

$500,000 per annum are much more likely to describe their jobs in the industry as agent or representative than women earning greater than $500,000. For example, one-third of women earning annual incomes between $200,000 and $499,999 describe their current job as agent or representative while only 17.6 percent of those earning between $500,000 and $999,999 describe themselves in this way. Why? In part this is due to length of service in the industry. As women and men mature in the industry, more of their income comes from previous production. Also, the more years they are in practice, the more designations they are likely to earn, and the more likely they are to incorporate more lines of business and service into their practices. Holistic planning requires more knowledge, experience, and licenses. Consequently, becoming a holistic planner may require more seniority. Since more years in practice often equates to higher levels of income, it is not totally surprising that more women at the highest levels of income describe themselves as holistic planners than at lower levels of income.

It appears from both the 2012 WIFS survey and the interviews of successful women conducted for this book that holistic financial planning is more likely to lead to higher levels of financial success than other financial services business models. However, it is important to note that it is not only holistic planners who are successful in the financial services industry—it is also women who focus on insurance planning and corporate benefits. Of the successful women interviewed for this book, four work only with risk-based insurance products. Another is in the corporate and employee benefits market. Others started their careers in insurance, but as their businesses grew and the industry changed, many of them moved from insurance planning only to comprehensive financial planning, including insurance and investments, often without changing companies.

## SUCCESSFUL WOMEN KNOW AND CAN ARTICULATE WHO THEIR CLIENTS ARE

One of the things that may separate the women featured in this book from women and men who are not as successful or highly compensated in the financial services industry is the ability to quickly respond to one of the following: Describe your A-plus client. Describe your ideal client.

These women know who their clients are today and who they want them to be in ten years. Less highly compensated women, as shown by the data in the 2012 WIFS study, are less able to articulate who their clients are and who they will become. Of course, the ability to know one's client comes partially from experience. However, it is important to note that the women in this study and the most highly compensated women responding to the WIFS survey are also planners. They plan for themselves as well as their clients. The planning they do for their businesses requires them to determine who their clients are today and who their clients will be in five to ten years. Without an understanding of how their clients will change, their businesses cannot grow.

Women and men who do not make business plans are not likely to be able to articulate with whom they currently work and how their client base will change over the years. Because the very successful women interviewed for this study know who their clients are and who their clients will be in the future, they can also tell you how their business models are likely to change. It was because these women understood the changing needs of their clients that their business models changed from insurance and risk-based planning to more holistic financial planning and wealth management. Business planning, therefore, is one of the key common elements of a successful business.

It is also clear from the 2012 survey and the in-depth interviews for this book that the majority of women in the financial services industry with the highest levels of compensation (more than $500,000 per annum) have clients with significant salaries and assets. Income and assets go hand in glove with the need to develop a financial plan, invest wisely, protect income and assets from loss, give to charity, and provide a legacy. Hence it is no surprise that women with high-net-worth clients are more likely to become holistic planners since meeting the client's needs is a primary goal of their practices.

Women who are most likely to describe themselves as wealth

managers, financial planners, or financial advisors tend to express their A-plus clients in terms of

- income (net or gross);
- investable assets;
- liquid assets; and
- net worth.

Most of the successful women in this study have—and seek—clients with net annual incomes of at least $350,000 or gross incomes of at least $1,000,000. Some suggest that this can represent the combined income of a couple, but most express it in terms of individual income. The investable assets or liquid assets of their A-plus clients range from more than $400,000 to more than $3,000,000. The net worth of these ideal clients ranges from more than $1,000,000 to at least $8,000,000 for executives or $12,000,000 for business owners. Those women who work in the retirement market usually seek retirees with more than $1,000,000 in investable assets. Some women who work in the closely held business market also articulate the annual revenue of their clients' businesses. Most of the women require an annual business revenue of more than $5,000,000.

Some of the women indicate the ideal age range for their clients: from under forty-five to seventy, for example. Those women in the business market may express the ideal size of the business in terms of number of employees: from ten to one hundred, for example. A few of the women indicate the assets under management (AUM) and/or the annual revenue flow, which is acceptable from each client—for example more than $500,000 AUM to $30,000,000 AUM, or a minimum of $25,000 of insurance premium per year.

Some successful women describe their clients based on traits critical for a financial planning business. These women include the financial, social, or business habits of their clients in their descriptions of the ideal client—for example

- interested in family and community;
- *c-level* executives or other senior management;

- good financial habits;
- suddenly single women of wealth;
- professionals and physicians; and
- great source of referrals.

Three of the women financial planners describe their clients in terms of character traits, rather than finances. Pamela Gilmour says:

> I don't have investment minimums, but I do require atti-
> tude minimums of my clients. This means being engaged
> in the planning process, doing the homework, respond-
> ing to our communications, and making decisions in a
> timely manner.

She further describes her ideal clients as "open minded and healthy." She likes working with the "under forty-five crowd" because "we have time on our side."

Melanie Shanty, who says she works primarily with Middle America, provides a bullet-pointed narrative description of her ideal clients:

- We have to genuinely like and care about the client and the client's financial well-being.
- There is an ongoing, average annual revenue goal per client of
  $2,000.
- The client has to be willing to participate in the planning practice, and for the most part, follow the direction and advice that
  we provide. This direction and advice is collaborative in nature
  and involves negotiation with the client to achieve a favorable
  financial outcome.
- The client is willing to be an advocate for the practice and where
  appropriate refer their family and friends.

Lisa Sappenfield Boyer has recommended financial minimums or requires that clients commit to investing 7 percent of their income per year. But she, like Melanie and Pamela, also has key traits and habits that she requires of her clients. The clients must

- value my opinion and advice;
- not be influenced by financial media;
- be willing to cooperate in a timely manner to correspondence from my staff or me; and
- be eager to refer me to people who fit this profile.

As before, it is important to note: Not all of the successful women featured in this book work only with affluent clients. However, all of the women can articulate who their clients are. Two of the highest-compensated women participating in the interviews for this book focus on a very different demographic. Their business models dictate that they work with people of all means and provide most risk-based insurance products to protect individuals, families, homes, automobiles, and businesses. These women are not only personal producers; they are also the leaders of large agencies with many agents.

The women who do not describe themselves as wealth managers, financial planners, or financial advisors have broader descriptions of their ideal clients. As Ellie Mills says of her clients:

> [They] range from poverty level to the affluent. While we can help all levels, our A-plus client is one that cares about [her or his] family's financial future and is willing to take action to help protect and plan for it.

Nancy Wolfe-Smith says of her agency's clients: "They are from all walks of life, in every class and ethnic group."

Typically the women who are the agents of full-service insurance agencies, those that provide most insurance products from health insurance to auto insurance, describe their clients as middle class. Also, the women who work primarily in life or disability insurance serve *working-class* clients from across the economic spectrum. The common value of their clients is that they care about protecting their families. Although the business models of these women are quite different from their wealth management colleagues, they are equally successful.

## TYPICAL WORKDAYS AND WORKWEEKS OF HIGHLY SUCCESSFUL WOMEN ARE MODELS OF EFFICIENCY AND FLEXIBILITY

How many hours a day or days per week these women give to their financial services businesses varies based on how long they have been in the business, whether or not they have business partners, the team and staff they hire, how their businesses are organized, and whether they are continuing to grow the businesses. All of the women interviewed for this book value flexibility, and many—particularly those who have had the same business model for many years—now take more time away from their businesses for family or other interests, particularly charitable ones.

Betty Harris Custer and her daughter Genevieve
rooting for their favorite football team.

Many of these women have worked with strategic coaches. (Strategic

Coach® is the registered trademark of business coach Dan Sullivan. Dan Sullivan and his team of coaches, including Colleen Bowler, who is featured in this book, work with some of the most successful business people in the country.) Strategic coaches assist business owners in organizing their time for peak efficiency. Strategic coaching also entails hiring of staff and developing key professional relationships that allow the women to focus on what they do best—while others perform other necessary tasks. The most typical business week for many of these women has three days devoted primarily to client appointments: Tuesday, Wednesday, and Thursday. Frequently, Monday is for team meetings, planning, and meeting with strategic partners. Friday is devoted to the most important client meetings (often getting the check), tying up the work of the week, and, for many, leaving the office early.

The women can keep this kind of a schedule because they have team members, strategic business partners, and corporate support, planning, and advisory groups, most often within their companies. These partners, team members, and support groups do research, complete client plans, and draft recommendations. Other team members manage their client base and calendar, do marketing and public relations, deal with paperwork and underwriting, service technology, and keep the office running smoothly. Frequently, these successful holistic planning women do a great deal of joint work with other financial and legal professionals, within their companies and outside. The keys to making the best strategic use of her time are business planning, staffing, and surrounding herself with the best possible professionals to service her clients. This allows the primary financial planner, including many of the women featured in this book, the time to work directly with her clients.

Some of the women who focus on holistic planning have been in the business for decades. Several have partners. At the time of their interviews, two had adult children who have joined them in the business. For these women, time away from the office may be as important as time in the office. Many consider their time working with charities in the local community as important to their businesses and their own personal well-being as it is to the community. Others seek personal and family time. Some do not come into the office until late in the morning or early in the afternoon each day; others take a week off per month or a long vacation each year. Still others devote their time to major company or professional organization leadership positions. Those with young children, of course, still blend motherhood and work each day. These younger women may have to wait until their children are older before they can personally benefit from the strategic business plans they have made.

## WOMEN DESIGN AND MAINTAIN A COMFORTABLE OFFICE

The ah-ha moments in life are not so much great surprises as they are obvious things that slap us in the face, make us stand up and take notice, and say, "Ah-ha!" Of course, I knew that all along." And, that's how it was for the authors of this book when the incredibly successful women they interviewed told them how much their office spaces have contributed to their business success.

With the large number of home design magazines on the market and the popularity of HGTV, the importance of well-designed office space to women should be no surprise. Although the authors never asked these women about their offices, many of the women told them anyway. The office environments that have helped these women achieve success involve not only how the office looks, although that certainly is important, but more critically how it functions to encourage client comfort and security as well as team productivity and *fun*. For younger women with children, quality office space provides places where their children can blend into their business day. It is clear from these women's comments about their businesses that the happiness and optimism of their team members is critical to the service they provide their clients and the success of the business. Several of the women include having fun as a team as one of their ongoing objectives. A well-designed office can help people feel secure, confident, and happy. As Nancy Wolfe-Smith says:

> Our office is fun, welcoming, engaging, and available. We are always finding new ways to make our clients comfortable and happy. Our extended office hours and Spanish-speaking team members open doors for many

clients who otherwise would not be helped by a State Farm agent. We invite our clients in at every phone inter-action because we know that they will feel at home and want them to return and bring their friends.

Fourteen of the twenty-three successful women interviewed for this book have their own offices outside of agency or corporate offices. For many of these women, having their own office space is an important key to their success. Several of them mention that their clients must feel comfortable and secure in the office. One of the women comments that her team members do not work in cubbies, but she provides workstations for her clients. This gives them a private space to do work while they wait or access their financial information prior to or during meetings.

Cubbies and workstations are the norm for most corporate and agency offices today. They may be efficient and cost effective, but for most of these women, they are impersonal and not conducive to developing the teamwork their clients expect and need if their businesses are to succeed. One woman commented that leaving the agency office sooner was the one thing that could have led to her earlier success. Office space (how it looks and how it functions) is critical to how these successful women conduct their business.

$$\approx$$

There are several things that all of these successful women do that if they did not do them they would not be as successful. These are the things that less successful women and men are less likely to do, thereby limiting their chance of success. Below is a summary of what these successful women do:

- They plan for all phases of their businesses, from what they expect to accomplish this year and in ten years to how they will transition their businesses into their retirement.
- At the center of all their plans are their clients and helping them achieve their financial goals.

- They know their clients well, and they respect them:
  - financially
  - as family members
  - as business people and professionals
  - as individuals
- They expect as much from their clients as they expect from themselves, and they communicate these expectations to their clients, including requiring clients to help them grow their businesses through referrals.
- They are leaders who attract successful, optimistic, and honest business associates and partners (in and outside of their offices) who can benefit their clients through the work they do jointly.
- They are team leaders who like and appreciate their team members and empower them to do high levels of work for their clients.

Juli McNeely (center) and her team who have helped make her multiyear commitment to leadership of NAIFA possible.

- They reward their clients by providing honest advice and doing the best possible work on their behalf.
- They reward their team members by providing them with benefits and appropriate compensation for the work that they do.

- They create office environments that are comfortable, productive, safe, and fun for clients, associates, family, and team members.

# CHAPTER 7 —————————————
# PAYING IT FORWARD AND GIVING BACK

> Learn more about the emotional impact of the outcomes [of the financial services business], not just the financial part—people's lives are truly affected by the work we do or don't do. Know what that means, up front. I didn't connect with this for some time. I was so busy learning *stuff* and so young. I didn't understand the mature aspects of what I was doing ... [I am] thankful for organizations like the **LIFE Foundation** [that] promote real-life stories and give us all better insights of the value of our work and time.
>
> —Robelynn H. Abadie, Abadie Financial Services, LLC, CAP®, RFC, LUTCF, CHRS®, CSA

## YOU CAN'T DO IT ALONE

All of the successful financial services professional women interviewed for this book recognize that they cannot run their businesses on their own. As State Farm agent and business owner Nancy Wolfe-Smith says, "It takes a village to run a business." They also know that they would not have been successful without the help of many—in and out of their offices, agencies, and companies. The small acts of kindness and big leaps of faith have helped them become who they are today.

One of the most remarkable traits of each of the twenty-three women featured in this book is the commitment to *paying forward* the help she was given by family members, friends, and professionals. In addition, these women give back to their clients, going above and beyond what is expected of them. They also give back to their companies and the industry, serving on boards and in many time-consuming leadership positions. These women are committed to their communities and work tirelessly to raise money and provide service for thousands of people less fortunate than they are. And there is not a woman among them who is not making it possible for young women (and men) to succeed in this industry through the friendship, mentoring, and leadership they provide. Successful women such as the ones featured in this book are literally changing the face and shape of the financial services industry with their commitment to integrity, teamwork, education, service, charity, and passion for excellence. This inspirational chapter will tell the stories of many of them.

## PAY IT FORWARD REQUIRES A THIRD-PARTY BENEFICIARY

The concept of paying it forward has been around for centuries. However, the term was coined recently. A 2000 movie by that name starring Helen Hunt, Kevin Spacey, and child star Haley Joel Osment gained limited critical acclaim, but it started a national phenomenon.[33] Based on a book of the same title by Catherine Ryan Hyde,[34] *Pay it Forward* spawned numerous other books of similar titles, a challenge and giveaways on the then mega-popular television show the *Oprah Winfrey Show*, and the "Pay It Forward Foundation," founded by the book's author.[35] What does paying it forward mean?

Paying it forward requires a third-party beneficiary. The simplest examples are what have become known as random acts of kindness, such as stopping to help a stranded motorist change a flat tire on her car along a busy stretch of road. The motorist, thankful for the help and mindful that not everyone would do it, sees an elderly woman drop her shopping bag a few days later. That thankful motorist goes to the lady's aid, stoops down to pick up the groceries, and places them in the bag. She even goes the extra mile of carrying the bag to the lady's car. Three people—two beneficiaries. The third-party beneficiary, the elderly lady, has no idea that her helper was helped by a passing motorist just a few days before. The two acts of kindness are selfless; neither the passing motorist nor the tire-changing beneficiary has any expectation that their kindness will be returned. However, when the first beneficiary (the motorist) acts out of kindness to the third-party beneficiary (the elderly lady), the act of kindness has been paid forward.

Most of the women appearing in this book talk about the help they were given early in their careers by managers, colleagues, family, friends, professionals they met briefly at meetings, or speakers they happened to hear. The bearer of the gift may not even know she or he has given it. However, the beneficiary, the new financial services professional, remembers it for many years and thinks of it again when she decides to say or do something kind to help a new financial professional who becomes the third-party beneficiary.

Donna Patton, for example, remembers receiving the occasional *at-ta-girl* notes from a vice-president of the Principal. She has paid it forward many times over the years by passing that simple act of kindness on to others.

According to Colleen Bowler:

> As for the people who have helped me, just thinking of all of them could make me cry. This is an industry where people are so willing to give.

## WHY DOES THE PUBLIC VIEW THE FINANCIAL SERVICES INDUSTRY LESS FAVORABLY?

Is this what consumers are likely to say about financial services professionals? Is this the picture painted by the media in advertisements, news stories, television shows, and films? Not likely. More often, professionals in the financial services industry are portrayed as money-grubbers who are willing to sell or promote anything as long as it is profitable for them—and, by extension, their companies.

Companies in the industry do not fare any better. Insurance is often looked at by consumers, including those who own it, as something that is expensive and often does not keep the promises that are made. Advisory firms are frequently portrayed in advertisements, sometimes by competitors within the industry, as taking hard-earned money and charging large unnecessary fees to invest it in ways that are not appropriate for the client.

Are these negative portrayals a fair picture of the financial services industry? Of course not, but unfortunately, the criticisms have been earned by abuses that have occurred throughout the industry in recent years. In part because of the significant amount of money that can be made as a financial services professional, the career does attract some individuals whose only motive is to make as much money as possible for themselves rather than for their clients.

However, the real picture of the industry is far less gloomy. In fact, the real picture is very clear and bright. Most of the professionals in the financial services industry are honest and hardworking, and they frequently pay it forward. The majority of the companies keep the promises they make to their customers. Most advisors fairly earn the fees and commissions they are paid. Many advisors who belong to professional organizations or receive professional designations take oaths of fiduciary service (similar to physicians and attorneys). Many professional designations require that the professional take numerous courses and pass difficult tests; demanding ethics courses are usually an important part of the curriculum. Every financial advisor is required to take and pass ethics continuing education courses each year, and companies include ethics in educational and training programs. Companies that discover an advisor or representative who is violating ethical codes severely punish the person and often dismiss her or him. Sometimes, the individual loses her or his licenses and can no longer practice.

Ethical behavior and an advisor's fiduciary responsibility to clients are taken seriously. Of course, this does not mean that every advisor is ethical. However, the vast majority are. It is the few who are unethical and featured in media reports that give the public the false impression that financial services is an industry of money-grubbers. The women featured in this book show how this image of the industry is untrue and unfair. In most cases, the exact opposite is true. The industry is peopled by women and men who *pay forward* and *give back* to their families, friends, other professionals, the industry, their communities, and—most importantly—their clients.

## GIVING BACK IS THE MANTRA OF SUCCESSFUL FEMALE FINANCIAL SERVICES PROFESSIONALS

The successful financial services professionals featured in this book represent the best of the industry. Not one of the twenty-three women interviewed for this book focused on how much she earns. Instead, each of these women talked about always doing what is in the best interest of her clients, even when the recommendation she makes is not in her best financial interest. Each of these women is equally focused on how much she has been given and on helping her colleagues, team members, and young recruits become as successful as she is. No jealousy or envy here. Selfless acts of kindness abound.

Certainly each of these women is proud of her success, including her financial success. However, she views her success in terms of good work done, not in terms of dollars earned. Each of these women recognizes how much she has been *given* by others and by the industry. She also believes that because she has been given a great deal, she must give back in time, knowledge, and money to the industry, her company, her team members, young professionals, her community, and her family. What she gives back is what has been paid forward on her behalf by all who have made a positive contribution to her professional and life journeys. Her commitment to giving back shapes how she does her business, often in surprising ways.

## SUCCESSFUL WOMEN PAY IT FORWARD AND GIVE BACK TO REPAY THOSE WHO HAVE GIVEN TO THEM

Almost every woman featured in this book comments on how important her early involvement in professional organizations has been to her professional development. According to Robelynn Abadie:

> My early involvement in industry volunteerism really helped carve the way for me. I wasn't from a family of insurance agents [or] had anyone close to me that was one. I had to figure all of this out for myself. Being around

other successful agents, even outside of my initial career agency, really helped me. I got a broader view of the
industry.

Robelynn goes on to talk about some of the important professionals
who believed in her and helped her learn what she needed to do in order
to become the successful professional she is today. She is grateful for the
woman with whom she worked in her first job in the insurance industry
selling cancer insurance. From that woman and their politically well-con-
nected boss, she learned about networking, selling, and how to run large
enrollments.

While she was still selling a large number of cancer policies, the man
who was to become her first professional manager in the industry called
her and asked, "How would you like to be in the insurance business?"

Robelynn was at first "put off" and said, "I am in the insurance business." In recalling this, she chuckles and says, "How wrong I was. All I
knew was a couple of cancer and dread disease policies ... the extent of
my insurance knowledge."

But because he persisted in encouraging her to become a career agent,
she decided to proceed with the interviews and tests. After a few months,
she was offered her first career agent contract. She is grateful that he did
not give up on her and even more appreciative of the opportunities he
provided that allowed her to deepen her understanding of what the career
could be.

These early experiences and the helpful, encouraging people who
made it possible for these women to overcome the difficult first few years
in the business are why they are committed to paying forward the help
and encouragement they received. As Toni Espey says, "Many times in
my life, I think back to the opportunity I was given and try as much as I
can to pay it forward to others." She gives an example of one such time
early in her career. She had been working as an adjuster for State Farm. A
year into this job, she and her husband decided to move to Florida.

My claims manager at the time found out that I was trans-
ferring with the company to Florida. He sat me down and

explained the opportunities of becoming an agent. He had no idea that becoming an agent was my goal. Then he made the introduction to his good friend [later to become her division manager in Florida]. It's a small world and connections are important. I don't believe a lot in chance. There are reasons why people show up in your life at a certain time. We just have to be smart enough to take advantage of those moments.

Further, these women would say, "Chance does not happen by chance." Chance and good luck are things these and other successful people prepare for. If Toni had not been doing an excellent job as an adjuster, her manager would not have referred her to her future district manager. And perhaps, her claims manager was also paying forward a connection someone helped him make in the early days of his career.

## MENTORING AND TEAM BUILDING ARE WAYS TO PAY IT FORWARD

How do these women pay forward all they have been given? Almost all of them mentor young women and men just starting their careers in the industry. Some of these new professionals are their own children, but most are not. Many of the women have identified their mentees with the help of professional organizations such as MDRT and WIFS.

Gail Linn, for example, has volunteered through MDRT, WIFS, and her company to be a mentor for young or new financial service professionals. She says that it is important for her to give back all the many kindnesses she has received during her career. For the service she has provided to the industry, Gail was awarded the 2014 WIFS Angel Award.

These women also pay it forward by helping their team member grow so that one day they may have their own successful careers in the industry and thereby assist future new financial services professionals in growing their careers. In this way, these women are helping attract and retain more like-minded people, particularly women, into the industry.

Ellie Mills actively mentors her team members. She helps each set professional goals and rewards them when their goals are achieved. One of Ellie's personal goals is helping as many team members as possible achieve the success she has achieved as a leader in her company. In her company this means putting "their own names on the door" of their own agencies.

Gail Linn, recipient of the 2014 WIFS Angel Award. The annual Angel Award recognizes a woman who has given back to the financial services industry.

The women interviewed for this book do not think of helping others become successful as creating competition. They view it as a way to pay it forward, build their own businesses, and provide a legacy.

Ellie Mills, head of table, and members of her team celebrate the promotion of one of the Mills' team members at a special luncheon. All of the team members attending the luncheon either met or exceeded their quarterly goals.

## GIVING BACK IS A PERSONAL AND BUSINESS VALUE FOR SUCCESSFUL WOMEN

The résumés of these women provide insight into the importance of service and charitable work in their careers and lives. How can they possibly have time to give back so much and so often? The answer lies in their motivation for giving and in how giving back changes and grows their businesses.

They blend their family lives into their businesses, and they integrate their lives of service with their business lives. All of them recognize how much they have been given and believe the aphorism "to those who have been given much, much is expected." However, they also understand that one does not separate what one gives from the life one lives. It is by giving that they have grown as individuals and as professionals. In fact, for many of them, their giving philosophy has framed their businesses.

Betty Harris Custer decided many years ago that giving up participation in her children's activities and charitable work was "too high of a price to pay" to become the first female Agent of the Year for Lincoln Financial. Instead, she has been satisfied to stay in the top fifty of the company's producers and maintain all her other activities. Today, those charitable activities, which take up many pages on her résumé, are central to her business model. "Our client base consists of individuals, family trusts, businesses, nonprofit entities, private foundations, local and state-wide charitable endowments, [and] retirement plans."

When discussing the portfolios of their clients she comments: "A significant portion of these portfolios has socially responsible concerns." Her husband, who joined her in the business twenty-six years ago, focuses much of his business on "socially responsible investing and alternative investment solutions." Betty says, "I am extremely involved in the community, spending upwards of fifteen to twenty hours a week on boards and in activities related to them."

As discussed in another context, Pamela Gilmour gives back by personally earning tens of thousands of dollars each year for the Alzheimer's Association, Leukemia Society, and Boy Scouts, and she has made it a value of her company to give back. Each of her team members and employees is expected to pick a volunteer activity and become engaged in it. In addition to the money she earns for charities, Pamela served on the board of trustees of the Baltimore Opera Company and has been president of the local Executive Women's Golf League.

Monica Jones, a member of the WIFS national board, is still relatively new to the financial services business. She has worked for a number of years in a feeding-the-homeless program through her temple. She also mentors Latina girls—ages twelve to eighteen—as she has for the past fifteen years. According to Monica, I have "a passion for helping these young women to look into their futures, have high expectations, thrive for success, and finish college." A Latina herself, she sets an example for these girls while she helps them become the best they can be.

Helping children is important to many of these women. Colleen O'Donnell Bowler has coauthored a book titled *Generous Kids: Helping Your Child Experience the Joy of Giving*.[36] The book was written to help parents and other adults teach children the habit of giving, according to Colleen, just as they are taught the habit of brushing their teeth. The Amazon summary of the book, which one reviewer calls "life-changing," says:

[It is a] simple book [that] will help parents make giving a fun and fulfilling part of their children's lives through learning the habit of giving. It's an easy-to-read book full of entertaining and practical suggestions, amazing true stories, simple examples, and plenty of *We can do that too!* takeaways for busy moms and dads.

Colleen Bowler (second from right), author of *Generous Kids*, with her family.

Robelynn Abadie spends much of her time in foundation and professional association leadership work, encouraging others to give back as she has. In 2010, she served as international president of the Million Dollar Round Table Foundation (MDRT). She sets an example for other financial representatives in terms of giving back by being an Excalibur Society member of the foundation, a recognition that honors the financial gifts she has given. She is past president of the Planned Giving Council of Greater Baton Rouge, Louisiana. She has served on the board of the Rotary Club Foundation and the National Association of Health Underwriters Education Foundation. She was national president of the Association of Health Insurance Agents (AHIA), and in 2002, she was the national president of WIFS.

Robelynn's community spirit was clearly exhibited following the devastation of Hurricane Katrina and Hurricane Rita. She served as a pediatric assistant at the Louisiana State University Maravich Center, the largest acute-care field house operation in the history of the United States. Hundreds of financial services industry friends used her office as a clearinghouse for tons of goods distributed to shelters. She also raised $110,000 to build a playground near the first evacuee trailer park in Baker, Louisiana.

Robelynn Abadie cutting the ribbon at the dedication of the playground she helped to build following Hurricane Katrina near Baker, Louisiana.

## A SUCCESSFUL WOMAN'S DESIRE TO PAY IT FORWARD AND GIVE BACK AFFECTS HER BUSINESS MODEL

For Robelynn Abadie, giving back and seeing the amazing results of her charitable work has moved her to change her business model after thirty-six years in the corporate benefit's business. As discussed previously in a different context, Robelynn now has two focus areas in her business: corporate benefits and charitable giving. She plans to sell her very successful benefits business within the next three to five years so that she can concentrate on charitable giving, particularly through permanent life insurance. To prepare for this change, she has earned the designation Chartered Advisor in Philanthropy (CAP®) and has worked at networking with other professionals in the charitable giving and estate planning fields.

Karen DeRose and her associates include giving back in the company's objectives because they recognize how their involvement in these socially conscious organizations helps build their business, which they describe as a "core values approach to planning. Life happens ... plan for it!'" One of their objectives is "promoting the Collaborative Law Fellowship for divorce planning." Another is a "sponsorship through the *Legal Balance* in the female law community in Chicago."

Another good example of how giving back influences these women's businesses is Gail Linn's work to educate women about finances and insurance. She and nine other women joined together to form the Brooklyn Regional Professional Women's Group. They decided the best way to educate women was through educational seminars in different venues throughout the region. She says of these efforts that occurred early in her career, "I found my voice and realized that this was my passion." Giving these seminars also convinced her of the importance of getting more education herself, so she enrolled at NYU to take courses and earn a CFP® designation.

Melanie Shanty's personal life, social commitment, and business have been united due to personal experience. For fourteen years, following the death of her mother, Melanie was the trustee of a special needs trust for her sister. "It was a daunting task and required professional skills." The recognition of this need and the understanding that "many families endure similar circumstances" led her to turn an outside business activity into an important part of her core business. She now consults with families who have loved ones with special needs. The focus of the financial planning she does with these families is to provide the resources they need to establish a continuum of care for when their loved ones are no longer able to provide that support themselves.

## SERVICE PROVIDED TO THE INDUSTRY IS ANOTHER WAY THESE WOMEN PAY IT FORWARD AND GIVE BACK

Many of these women serve leadership roles in their companies and in the industry to pay forward what they were given by other professionals as they were getting started in their careers. These women learned early that surrounding themselves with positive, helpful colleagues was important to their success. Some of the women found these professionals in their offices, agencies, and companies. Others sought these associations through professional organizations such as MDRT, WIFS, and NAIFA. The assistance and encouragement these professionals gave these women when they were most vulnerable during the early years of their careers helped them become the successful businesswomen they are today. Likewise, it convinced them of the importance of being supportive to each new generation of financial services professionals. As Robelynn Abadie says:

> In my thirty-six years as an agent [and] advisor, I can recount numerous stories of women [and] men who engaged me, supported me, were there at the right time, lifted me up, pushed me forward, and just told me I could do this. They seemed to appear at the perfect moments in time.

Below is a sampling of what these women have done in service to the industry and their companies.

Several of the women featured in this book have served in major leadership positions in professional financial services organizations. The extensive time they have invested in these organizations has not only benefitted the organizations but has helped these women leaders grow their businesses often in surprising ways. Gail Linn was the president of the Financial Planning Association of New York (FPANY) in 2013 and chair of the board in 2014. She says that her leadership has led to opportunities to speak and meet with many leaders in the industry.

According to Gail:

> Since the financial services industry is still young and transitioning, I have always felt obligated to play a role in shaping its future. It is important to step up and volunteer so that I can have a part in helping the next generation continue the mission of financially educating the public. Stepping up to positions of leadership helps build confidence, which is needed to be successful in the business.

Both Robelynn Abadie and Kathleen Godfrey have served as president of WIFS. Kathleen reports that during her tenure as president, her business skyrocketed. "My bottom line was up 35 percent even though I was traveling all the time. It forced me to be a better time manager, and it really increased my confidence."

Kathleen Godfrey wielding a hammer for Habitat for Humanity.

In September 2014, Juli McNeely became the first female president in NAIFA's 125-year history. She says of this endeavor:

For two and a half years, I [have been] extremely busy speaking across the country to media outlets and working to defend our industry. I will say that my involvement in NAIFA has been a huge addition to my personal and professional life. I certainly give a significant amount of my time to this role, but I receive so much back in return: connecting with other successful advisors and sharing sales ideas and practice management strategies. I have also reaped a benefit I did not anticipate: a PR (public relations) exposure far beyond my community.

## FINANCIAL SERVICES COMPANIES HAVE BENEFITED FROM THE LEADERSHIP OF HIGHLY SUCCESSFUL WOMEN

Many of these women have served leadership roles within their companies. Some have been the first females to serve in these roles. Betty Harris Custer was the first female regional manager at Investors Life/ INA in 1979 and the third female regional manager at Lincoln Financial Advisors in 1996. She has served as a member of Lincoln Financial Advisors' high achievers' Chairman's Council and is a life member of the Resource Group, composed of Lincoln's top financial planners.

Anne Machesky, also with Lincoln, is currently vice chair and will become chair of the Resource Group next year. As a board member of the Resource Group, Anne chaired the investment committee for five years. She was also a managing principal for Lincoln in Minneapolis while she continued to run her own successful practice. She did this during a time when she says, "LFA was in a difficult transition." She saw her role "as taking care of the family of advisors and holding the office together." Although she left her leadership position after two years to concentrate on her own practice, she says of the experience:

My business partner Jean Breider and I persevered through LFA's transition, honed our craft, brought more comprehensive planning back into our client relationships, and I was able to refine my role, skills, and interests to support tremendous business growth and deeper client relationships that still exist today.

Karen DeRose is the chairman of Lincoln's new Women's Advisory Board—The WISE Group—Women Inspiring, Supporting, and Educating female advisors and women clients. In addition, she is past chairman of Lincoln's Resource Group—TRG Top 200 advisors at Lincoln. The board's mission is to develop "top" deliverables and "best practices" for all planners at Lincoln Financial Network.

Gail Linn has served on the MetLife Women's Leadership Circle. Lisa Sappenfield Boyer was the first—and to this day only—female president of Transamerica's top producers' group. And Barbara Brazda Dietze has served on the New York Life Agents' Advisory Council.

≈

The time invested by these very successful women to give back to their communities, companies, and the financial services industry has opened doors for a future generation of women financial professionals. These successful women are models for how to succeed while selflessly paying forward the debt they owe to those professionals who helped them grow in the early years of their businesses. Also, these women give back what they have been given to their communities, companies, associations, and clients. All of them have learned through their commitment and service that giving back has grown their businesses and fulfilled their lives. For these women, perhaps the most important thing giving back has done is taught them how to better serve their clients every day. In many ways, their clients become the third-party beneficiaries as these successful female financial services professionals pay forward the many acts of kindness they have received.

# CHAPTER 8
# TRANSITIONS AND SUCCESSION

---

*Transitions*

After assessing the macro trends in financial planning back in 2000, I saw a need for refocusing, which required a broker-dealer change, to get back to comprehensive planning versus mostly wealth management.

After eighteen years of running my own RIA with another broker-dealer, the shift was big and very worrisome in 2001. My worries were: How would clients see the change? How would it disrupt my practice? How much financial risk was there to my business's income? Would the promises made by the new broker-dealer be kept? What risks was I not seeing or assessing?

There were many sleepless nights before I made the final business decision to change … in 2001. The switch was very stressful, moving a large, loyal client base. Many individual conversations were needed to clarify my core reasons.

Looking back, it was very risky but very worth it. My business success has become broader than I expected. My services are more comprehensive, and I serve a very diverse client base. I have better tools, support, and technology.

—Anne Machesky, Financial Planner, Sagemark
Consulting/Lincoln Financial Advisors

---

---

*Succession*

Succession ("building a long-lasting organization") . . . a challenge for sure . . . I have attempted three different times, bringing an advisor in to do joint work to see if values match. Three different reasons for the match not to work, but none of them did.

In talking with business advisors, they say it takes three to five times to make a good succession work, kind of like dating if you want the best outcome for you, your clients, your team, and the new owner. It may take one to two tries if money is the only issue (they say). I would say this is a distinction with women as more do tend to want to make sure it is a fit for all.

—Colleen Bowler, CFP®, Lincoln Financial
Advisors, Strategic Wealth Partners

---

## TRANSITIONS: CHANGE HAPPENS!

All of the women featured in this book have sustained many "transitions" during their careers in the financial services industry. Transitions that could affect one's business are either personal or professional.

The most difficult *personal transitions* may impact a woman's business more than a man's. A 2014 research study of Harvard Business School male and female alumni found the following:

> Men generally expect that their careers will take prece-
> dence over their spouses' careers and that their spouses
> will handle more of the child care—and for the most
> part, men's expectations are exceeded. Women, mean-
> while, expect that their careers will be as important as
> their spouses' and that they will share child care equally,
> but, in general, neither happens. This pattern appears to
> be nearly as strong among Harvard graduates still in their
> twenties as it is for earlier generations.[37]

These difficult transitions typically involve relationships and family. They include the following:

- marriage
- divorce
- death of a spouse
- childbirth
- parenting and child care
- grandchildren
- caregiving of parents, in-laws, and other family members

> My first professional transition came only months after entering the business as I became pregnant right after getting married, which is pretty much the same time I started in the business. Then I proceeded to have all three children from 1984–1989. My mentor and manager said I was good at production.
>
> —Lisa Sappenfield Boyer

For many of the women in this study, one of these difficult life passages caused them to change careers and enter the financial services business. Unfortunately, for other women, these personal transitions, often coupled with the lack of support of managers and spouses, cause them to exit the financial services industry's revolving door just as they are getting settled into the career.

## CHANGE IN MARITAL STATUS CAN CAUSE DISRUPTION IN BUSINESS

Three of the women featured in this book entered the business because of their husbands' sudden, tragic deaths. In two cases, the women were forced to face difficult financial issues. For both of these women, finding a career that would provide the income they needed to support the children and the flexibility required to work and raise a family were primary motivators for entering the industry. The third woman remarried before she entered the industry, but the death of her first husband and the loss of a business she and her second husband owned together made her realize how important insurance had been to her and her young family's survival. For her, it was as if the industry had reached out and said, "You are meant for this business."

Two other women, recently divorced and single mothers, had similar motivations for entering the industry: income potential and flexibility. Four other women divorced shortly after entering the business. In each case, they found their husbands not to be as supportive of their career choice as they had expected. For one woman, the divorce from an abusive husband, even though child support became totally her responsibility, made it easier to focus on her business and gave her the motivation she needed to succeed.

For all of these women, failure was not an option. They had no choice, at times in spite of their managers' comments to them that they would not succeed, but to pick themselves up and keep moving forward. And they did succeed, often beyond their wildest dreams, at times, surpassing all the male professionals in their agencies or offices.

However, success did not always mean that life's transitions were easy. Some of these women worked part-time while their children were young, but they came back full steam ahead as soon as they knew their children were safe and cared for. For some, juggling child care and work meant switching traditional family roles with their husbands as primary caregivers of the children and these women as primary breadwinners for the family. This change of traditional spousal roles also caused bumps in the road for some.

## JUGGLING AND BALANCING CHILDREN, MARRIAGE, AND BUSINESS CAN CREATE PROBLEMS IN ALL THREE

I have experienced a lot [of transitions] in my lifetime as a financial advisor. I became the main breadwinner early in my career, which actually inspired me to work hard. Lucky for me, I had the full support of my husband. It was not easy at first adjusting emotionally and financially . . . Once I finally accepted it, I realized that it did not matter who stayed home with the children as long as they were loved, taken care of, and we worked together as a team. It took us a while to figure that out, but we truly became a partnership and accepted each other's roles at that point in our lives, and we have both not looked back since.

—Karen DeRose

For others, juggling children and business meant finding school environments to nurture not only the children but the entire family. Others found ways to have their very young children in their offices—even though some of their managers were not supportive. Some hired help to care for the responsibilities of home and family. Whatever their solutions to the difficulties of raising their children while building a successful business, all of them put their children and the family first. If this meant missing an appointment, working from home, or making a change from their demanding entrepreneurial roles to jobs with paychecks, they made the adjustment. They learned to do what needed to be done without guilt. And, while doing what needed to be done, they found ways to continue to service their clients and rebound into their entrepreneurial roles as soon as possible. Sometimes rebounding meant partnering with other professionals, hiring staff, getting special dispensations from their companies, or even "defying the rules" to do what needed to be done to support their children, emotionally and financially, and serve their clients as well as they possibly could.

> The boys (twins) were born seven weeks early. Because I had my own office, I controlled my schedule. I actually took the boys into the office about half the time until they started preschool. My husband was a stay-at-home dad but still needed his time without the kids to do what we needed for the home. We had a nursery put into the office, and the boys grew up in the office. It slowed down my personal production but also gave me a wonderful conversation starter to talk about protecting your family!
>
> —Toni Espey

For these women, their children and families came first, but their clients' needs were always next. Some of the women in this study are still raising young children while building a business and are learning how to successfully juggle all their roles and responsibilities. It is not easy, and as many of them said in their interviews, it is difficult to find female mentors who have shared similar personal and professional experiences to provide the advice and encouragement they need.

Personally in forty-three years I have seen one marriage end, another begin, two children and three grandchildren resulting from that one. I lost both parents and a sister in that time. And I lost many friends. So I've gone the full cycle of life from single to married to divorced to married to family to empty nester to grandparent. I also was a major caregiver for my parents and two aunts. My husband and I have also provided significant support for two struggling brothers (one each) and for two adult children of a good friend who lost both parents at young ages.

—Betty Harris Custer

## BEING A CAREGIVER MAY CREATE BUSINESS CHALLENGES, BUT IT IS ALSO A WAY WOMEN GIVE BACK

Other women featured in this book discussed their roles as caregivers for adult family members and their pleasure in being able to do so. Because of the income and time flexibility a financial services career allows, particularly after many years in the business with a loyal client base, these women became the caregiver of family members and provided financial support.

Dianna Parker has not yet had to provide care for parents, but she built a guesthouse on her property so that if her parents need care, she and her husband will be able to provide it. The house has already been occupied by other family members going through their own life transitions. "I am very happy to be able to assist our family in ways I never would have imagined, and having a successful career in this profession has provided me with the opportunity to do that."

The biggest transition I faced in the past five years was supporting my mom as she battled cancer. She is in remission now, but she has battled it twice in the past five years (three times over her lifetime). My mom is single, so my sister and I were with her along the way. I was certainly grateful for the chance to be with her for her chemo, radiation, and doctors' appointments. The time we spent together was precious. My mom continues to battle health issues, and my sister and I will continue to be there for her.

—Juli McNeely

Many other women interviewed for this book comment that it is a privilege to be in a profession that gives them the financial ability and the time to help family members through difficult times in their adult lives. Lisa Sappenfield Boyer, whose father has had progressive MS for over fifteen years, is grateful to her husband for picking up more of the responsibility for their children as her business grew, giving her time to help her parents. She is also thankful that her career has given her the ability to help them with her time and financially.

Karen DeRose's husband, who provided care for their children while Karen was growing the business, is now providing care for his disabled sixty-three-year-old brother with pancreatic cancer and provided care for his ninety-three-year-old father until his recent death. They also help in their financial support. Karen says, "No one really counts on providing care or financial assistance for adult family members in their own planning." Karen is grateful that her business has allowed her husband and her to give this financial support and time to their family. She looks at this as paying back for what her mother-in-law paid forward many years ago.

> My mother-in-law took care of our children while we went to work each day and changed her work schedule to the night shift to be home with our children. She was an amazing woman. She took no money for taking care of our children, so now I feel [helping my husband's brother and the past help with my father-in-law] is our way of paying them back for all they sacrificed for us.

## TRADITIONAL FEMALE ROLES CAN CREATE BUSINESS CHALLENGES FOR WOMEN

The women featured in this book and a large percentage of all the women in the financial services industry have dealt with personal transitions that may have affected their lives more than similar transitions would have affected the lives of their male colleagues. Women who build successful careers in the industry have survived these transitions, and their businesses have thrived as they raised their children, became single parents, cared for aging parents, and gave countless hours to charities in their communities and in service to their companies and the profession.

Many of these women have weathered difficult personal issues, often without support, while growing successful businesses in an industry that has been and continues to be male dominated with few female role models or mentors. All of these women joined companies with leadership (according to CFP®/WIN research) that "still believe women—but not men—are apt to cut and run when it comes time for having children."

Although many of these women talk of the great respect they have for the men who have trained and mentored them, they also confirm what previous studies have shown: that their career paths would have been smoother if they had had other women to provide business and personal advice. The women featured in this book agreed to participate in a lengthy and time-consuming interview process because of their commitment to helping current and future generations of women in the profession.

## IF WE KEEP FOCUSED ON CREATING VALUE FOR THE CLIENT, WE ARE ALWAYS MOVING FORWARD

Most of the women interviewed for this book have gone through many business transitions, but all of them agree that by keeping their focus on what is best for the client, they get through these transitions successfully. Many of their work-related transitions have occurred because of personal life changes: marriage, death of spouse, divorce, parenting, spouse's career changes, illness of self or close family member, and others. However, some of their major business transitions are simply because they have been financial services professionals during a time of great tumult within the industry.

As mentioned in an earlier chapter, legislative changes have moved the financial services industry from individual companies dealing with a specific service or product to an industry focused on holistic financial planning through multiple products, investments, and services. It has been a time when companies have changed what they do and how they do it. Women who completed the 2012 WIFS survey, were interviewed for this book, and entered the career selling a single insurance product are now working in fields such as retirement, succession, and estate planning. Women who managed the wealth of their clients through investments are advising clients in all aspects of their financial lives, including protecting against risk. Companies are attempting to differentiate themselves. What do we do? How do we do it better than other companies? All of this has meant that these women have had to change what they do, gain new knowledge, and learn new skills to be able to serve their clients.

> You must be able to adjust to the many changes this business can throw your way, whether they are directed by outside forces (e.g., stock market, tax law changes) or internal forces (changes within company structure, change of target market, change of business activity).
>
> —Gail Linn

## MARKET, LEGAL, TAX, AND COMPANY CHANGES ALL AFFECT BUSINESS

At the same time, these women have had to work with their clients through a new financial crisis every few years. Women are likely to be as good as men in helping their clients through times of financial stress, but they may find it more challenging because of the value they place on always doing what is in the best interest of the client.

## INDUSTRY LEADERSHIP IS NOT CONVINCED WOMEN CAN SUCCEED—EVEN THOUGH THEY BELIEVE WOMEN ARE MORE LIKELY TO BE STRONGLY ETHICAL THAN MEN

All women in financial services have to weather their personal and business transitions as well as market, legal, and industry changes while working in an industry with leadership that is not convinced women can succeed. Only 7 percent of the leaders in financial services firms, according to the CFP®/WIN study, believe that women are more likely to have the characteristics of a successful financial planner than men. And 41 percent say that men are more likely to have the characteristics of successful financial planner than women. However, when these same leaders are asked about specific qualifications considered important for financial planners, women score higher than men. Notably, these leaders say that 88 percent of women financial planners are strongly ethical, as compared to 67 percent of male financial planners.[38]

The women featured in this book agree with this assessment; they often talk about unethical practices of some of their male managers and male colleagues, but not one mentioned the same lack of ethics in women. Of course, this does not mean that all men in the profession are unethical, and it does not mean that all women are ethical. In fact, in their interviews, these women were more likely to focus on the men who helped them build their businesses and cheered them along the way. Many of these women have male business partners and successors. However, these successful women agree that men are more likely than women to count their success in terms of the money they make and the company and industry recognitions they earn, which is usually based on production, than women are. Women judge their success in terms of the number of people whose lives are better because of the planning and risk-management work they have done.

## ALTHOUGH STUDIES SHOW THAT WOMEN MAY BE MORE RISK-ADVERSE THAN MEN, THE SUCCESSFUL WOMEN IN THIS STUDY ARE WILLING TO TAKE RISKS IN ORDER FOR THEIR BUSINESSES TO SUCCEED

The CFP®/WIN study suggests that women are *risk-averse* and less likely to change companies or career paths.[39] However, the successful women featured in this book are not risk-averse. In fact, they are risk takers when the risk is calculated to be in the best interest of their clients and their business. Here is what Colleen Bowler says about her business transitions:

> My path went from being a sole practitioner to hiring a half-time person, then a full-time person, then a cowork agreement with an advisor who did investments only while I did financial and estate planning. This lasted for about seven years ... Then back to just me ... Then hiring an employee financial planner who met with clients. That only lasted one year. And now I am bringing on someone who is an advisor, not an employee, whom I hope to mentor under my umbrella. I started with MONY for a year;

then transferred to Lincoln Financial. This has worked very well, offering independence with the depth of a big corporation. Managing transitions has never been very difficult … I learned long ago that change happens. Attitude makes a big difference. Change can be disruptive, but the goal is to keep focused on creating value for the client, and we are always moving forward.

Most of the women featured in this book have had numerous business transitions. Many were risky. The women were proactive and planned for the changes they were making. Even so, some of the transitions were not successful. Those that did not work as planned were not failures. Instead, they resulted in the women learning many new things that could be put to good use in subsequent business transitions.

Many of these very successful women have had several partnerships. Most were started to allow the women to gain new skills and provide additional services. Some of the partnerships worked and continue today, but most did not. The transitions were always difficult, and the needs of the client were always central to the decision to begin or dissolve a partnership.

Most of these women have also hired numerous staff members, typically called team members by the women. Some of these team members were professionals with credentials who the women hoped would one day become partners. Others served professional roles in their offices, such as developing financial plans, but did not meet with clients. Some did both: serving professional support roles and also meeting with clients. Every one of these transitions posed a financial, personal, and service risk for these women. However, the women did not hesitate to take the risk if they believed it would provide better information and service to their clients.

## NEW PARTNERSHIPS, CHANGING COMPANIES, AND ADDING PROFESSIONAL COMMITMENTS CAN BE VALUABLE, BUT THEY CAN ALSO BE RISKY

Karen DeRose has had three business partners; the first was her father. His retirement, Karen says, "forced me to stand up on my own."

Her father's business was strictly in insurance, but she transitioned the business to a planning practice. She then partnered with a CFP® who mentored her in financial planning. This relationship resulted in her earning her own CFP® designation at the age of thirty-five, having completed her first degree at thirty-two. Karen took classes and studied at night and worked full-time building the business during the day. Karen recalls those years of studying for her degree and her CFP® as grueling. "What was I thinking: raising kids, building a practice and now getting my CFP®? It was crazy but worth it!"

Karen DeRose, her father, and her son: three generations of financial planners.

Although Karen and her CFP® mentor continued as partners for several years, their philosophies about how to run a business differed, and they eventually parted ways. However, to this day, they share some clients and remain friends. She says that the breakup year was very difficult. However, like all the successful women in this book, even though the partnership did not succeed as planned, she benefitted and learned a great deal from it.

Her next and final partners, she hopes, are her son, Anthony, and Caitlin, the financial planning manager of Karen's practice. Caitlin plans to become a financial advisor in 2016. Now, with her son as her partner, Karen reports that her career has come full circle with three generations of financial planners in the family.

Pamela Gilmour worked with two different insurance agencies for fifteen years at the start of her career and then moved to a detached agency where she partnered with two male planners for eight years.

> Everyone was shocked that I left the agency to work with them, and I knew our value systems were not the same. However, I learned a lot about systems, sales, and customer service, and how *not* to run a practice and how *not* to treat clients and employees. Eighteen months before my two partners filed for bankruptcy, I went out on my own, as a detached agency. That was four years ago, and I have never been happier, and never looked back.

Melanie Shanty also has had numerous changes in how she has done her business. She began her career in the insurance industry, recruited by her CFP® mother, "long before the title was considered fashionable." Even though Melanie had no experience or education related to insurance, a Baltimore agency offered her a position as an advisor-trainer because of her mother's advocacy. She was given a two-year salary subsidy, which did not need be repaid as long as she met production requirements. She shared an office with another agent and participated in what she calls "an excellent eight-week training program." Five years into the business, she and her mother and sister formed a partnership under their own marketing name. Their goal was to formulate the beginnings of a financial planning practice. Her mother had been diagnosed with cancer and knew her time was limited:

> My mother wanted to leave her career having formed an organization with a much larger calling. She was passionate about retirement planning and felt that it presented an opportunity to step into the future and drive the conversation. She was correct. As I look back, I realize that the eight years I worked with her laid the foundation for me to form my own practice. She taught me how to navigate in what was mostly a man's world.

After her mother's death, Melanie and her business partner converted her mother's block of business in their names and purchased another practice in the marketplace. According to Melanie, purchasing that practice was a big financial risk. However, the practice they purchased had been hugely successful, and the advisor who owned it wanted to retire. They hired a practice manager and worked toward expanding their client base by offering what Melanie terms "robust planning services."

When Melanie realized the partnership was not working as she had planned, she split with her partner and opened her own practice and office with only her own personal clients and files. Melanie reports that the most fortuitous part of becoming a sole practitioner is that her son, just discharged from the marines, has joined her in her practice. Like Karen DeRose, Melanie and her son represent two of three generations in their financial services family.

Juli McNeely took a risk and changed her firm's broker-dealer. Doing so was very difficult and is something she never wants to do again. Also, she has had to let four staff members go over the years, which is never an easy task. However, she says she is proactive, anticipates transitions, and has a plan for the changes she makes.

Juli's biggest transition and potential risk to her business is also her greatest accomplishment. She is the first woman to go through the executive chairs of NAIFA to become the president of the largest professional organization in the financial services industry. To do this, she has had to adapt her practice to allow for the significant time commitment to this professional organization. As with her other business transitions, she has been proactive and planned for the changes that needed to occur in her business in order to continue to serve her clients and grow her practice while assuming leadership of NAIFA. Consequently, her years going through NAIFA's executive chairs have been beneficial to her, her clients, and her business. She has streamlined her book of business and reassigned clients to other advisors in her firm. She has made her practice more efficient so it can continue to operate whether she is in her office or on the road. Her travel responsibilities have increased each year as she has progressed through NAIFA's executive chairs.

According to Juli, focus is the key to her success. When she is at work, she is working. Without this focus, she says, "I could not do both." Now, as she completes her term as president of NAIFA, she can see the end of this professional commitment on the horizon. When she has a free moment, she dreams of how her business might grow when her commitment to NAIFA ends. She asks herself, "What will I do with all my free time?" She is considering a move toward fee-based advising. For years, her income has come totally from commission. This has been true since her father founded the firm. Fee-based advising would give her another stream of income and increase the value of her practice for succession planning purposes.

Many of the women in this study took field or corporate management positions at various times during their careers. Some of these transitions occurred because the women needed paychecks during personal or family crises. Others assisted their companies during the difficult transitional period following the repeal of the Glass-Steagall Act in 1999 when companies went from providing one type of financial product and service to providing multiple products and services to their clients. Other women accepted management positions in order to help their companies during corporate mergers that threatened the culture, important to the woman, of one of the two predecessor companies. The women who moved from personal production to management made the change while planning to return to their own businesses in the future. Therefore, they proactively negotiated with their companies to retain their personal clients, often by partnering with other professionals, and returned to their entrepreneurial practices as soon as practical. They knew these transitions would be difficult for themselves and their clients. Their primary consideration as they made these transitions was doing what was in the best interest of their clients. Money they might earn was not an important consideration. For all of them, they never lost sight of their primary goal. Dianna Parker calls this goal the creation of a "serve-first culture."

Although the women in this study have experienced many personal and business challenges leading to difficult transitions, they have succeeded. Betty Harris Custer says, "Every transition presented a challenge, but I always knew each challenge led to growth—and it did."

Paula Zonin makes a similar point with a bit stronger language, "Neither divorce, company mergers, or new general agents could knock me off my career path. I always stayed focused and self-motivated. This career allows you to reach as far as you desire!!"

Betty Harris Custer celebrates the good life at her home in Wisconsin.

## SUCCESSION: PLANS DIFFER DEPENDING ON THE TYPE OF BUSINESS

All of the women featured in this book are planners in the financial plans and advice they provide for their clients and in their businesses. It could be said that the more they plan, the more successful they become. However, for many of them, their most difficult plan lies ahead. *How do I find the person or people who have the same serve-first, client-centered values that I have to sustain my practice and work with my clients when I retire? How do I mentor and train them to serve my clients as I would? How do I allow them to use their unique skills to change my business model to their own while continuing to serve my clients as I have served them? How much is my business worth? Can I sell it? Do I want to sell it? How long and how much will I work?*

Unfortunately, the more that clients and team members become a part of the business sale equation, the more difficult it becomes to find a successor. However, for most of these incredibly successful women, succession and business continuation is a huge issue—and an even bigger opportunity. And even though they are all excellent planners, planning for their own successful succession may be more difficult than anything they have planned for previously.

## FOR SOME OF THE WOMEN, NO SUCCESSION PLAN IS POSSIBLE

With that said, a minority of the women featured in this book will have no succession plan. Their companies, typically in the insurance industry, do not allow it. Their general agents will decide or approve their successors. Their book of business will revert to the company. Their clients, even though they may view them as theirs, are actually clients of the company who may transfer them to other agents or service them as company or agency clients.

Some of these women will be able to select which of their clients will be transferred and to whom. However, these women have nothing to sell because their renewals and other fees are theirs and cannot be transferred to other agents. Their companies may use these renewals to fund the women's retirement plans. This certainly protects their retirements, but it may also add to their frustration as they try to ensure their clients are well cared for.

## SOME WOMEN MAY BE ABLE TO SELL A PART OF THEIR BUSINESS—BUT NOT ALL OF THEIR BUSINESS

For some, there is a middle ground. Juli McNeely has worked for commission only for most of her years in the business. Although she does not intend to retire for many years, she has already streamlined her client base and transferred her clients to other agents to give her the time she needs to serve out her executive terms with NAIFA. Juli, in many ways, has a head start on her succession. She reports, "I am working with a small, select group of clients."

When her tenure with NAIFA ends in 2015, she will be able to change her business model for new growth—and perhaps new streams of income. She has the time to build her practice to make it more saleable. She has already identified two, soon to be three, advisors in her firm who could successfully work with her clients. She also has a sixteen-year-old niece who has expressed an interest in the business. And since Juli is in a second-generation practice, she would love to have a family member succeed her. Her broker-dealer has a buyout loan option available to advisors that could allow one or more of them to purchase her practice. Since it has been only five years since she completed the succession of her father's business to her, she has her own succession on her radar, but she is not focusing on it yet.

Juli says, "I love what I do, but I am also open to what else may come next …" For the foreseeable future, Juli may be filling all the free time she will have after her NAIFA commitment to grow her business in ways that are today only a dream.

It is also true, that some of the women in this study who are agents of large insurance companies also have a "doing business as" (DBA) identity and/or "outside business activity" (OBA) ownership. The women with these market identities or ownerships may have more flexibility in transitioning their businesses and may even be able to sell all or a part of them. The brand created in the local marketplace may add to the value of the business and permit ease of transition that survives beyond the active practice of the agent/advisor.

## SOME WOMEN MAY CONTINUE TO WORK, BUT THEY REDUCE THEIR TIME COMMITMENT AND RESPONSIBILITIES

Some of the women who will not have succession plans may have the option to remain in senior status and continue to work, at the level they choose, with some or all of their clients. In some companies, senior status will allow these women to continue to receive renewals from products previously sold and other fees while working fewer hours, not adding new clients, not meeting any production minimums, and transitioning their business more slowly.

Toni Espey says she is a captive agent and does not own the policies she writes, but she services them and has several options as she approaches retirement. If she remains active in the business, she can have someone take over the day-to-day operations of the business and continue to receive her monthly commissions. This would allow her to slow down, remain as the agency decision maker, and continue to receive income.

Although not having to create a succession plan removes some of the pressure of transitioning into retirement, not having the flexibility to create their own succession plans may be more of a problem for female rather than male financial services professionals. The reason women often have difficulty in not having ownership of their clients is that they have always put their clients first and are concerned that as they transition out of the business, the promises they have made to their clients may not be kept.

## SUCCESSION REQUIRES A PLAN, A COACH, A LOT OF HELP, AND SOME GOOD LUCK

For many women who own their own businesses and work under the umbrella of a large corporate broker-dealer, a succession plan is a must. Other women, most of those with a DBA or OBA, also need a plan. Succession plans are complex. The women must take their successors into consideration.

In many cases, they must value their businesses in terms of what is saleable—and for how much. They must also determine how long and how much they plan to be involved in the business after the successor assumes primary responsibility for the business. Many of the women in this study, even those ten to fifteen years from retirement age, are mentoring team members or younger partners to be their successors. One of the problems faced by some of these women is that their long-time business partners will be retiring at approximately the same time as they will. If so, the succession plan must include the needs and desires of all the partners.

Many of the women interviewed for this book are approaching retirement and are working with succession advisors or coaches, just as they worked with or continue to work with strategic business coaches during the business-building process. And for some of these women, they are continuing to build their businesses even as they deal with succession issues. The better the business, the more there is to sell and the likelihood of finding a values-driven, client-centered, and qualified successor increases.

Many of the women recognize that finding one successor to replace them is unlikely—not because there are not good young professionals but because they have contributed so much to the business for so many years that their current value is far more than what a younger successor can contribute. Similarly, many of the women featured in this book are already mentoring one of their children or have children who are entering the profession and could become their successors. Although having one of your children succeed you in the business is the realization of a dream, it also adds to the complexity of the succession plan. If more than one professional will be needed to succeed the woman or her offspring is becoming her successor, continuing to build the business, even during preretirement years, is critically important. How do these women do it all? Here are some of their succession stories.

## BETTY HARRIS CUSTER
### CFP®, CRPC®, FOUNDING MANAGING PARTNER, CUSTER FINANCIAL SERVICE, LINCOLN FINANCIAL ADVISORS

No matter how hard we try, succession planning is rarely easy. Betty has brought at least four people into her business with a plan of making them successors. "For a variety of reasons the perfect fit has not been there." As she freely admits, finding a successor who fits "reflects as much on me as it does on them." Her husband and business partner of twenty-six years will be retiring at about the same time she does. She is comfortable staying in the business for another five to six years. She is healthy and has the flexibility to do the charitable work and visit her children and grandchildren as she pleases. She would "love to find a woman to be at least one of two prospective successors."

She is currently updating the valuation for her business, which was originally done five years ago. She says that financial professionals regularly solicit her about taking over her business, "but it is hard to find someone I think will do all I have done for my clients." This is the ongoing problem for successful female financial planners. Although all recognize that the financial piece is important, for successful female financial services entrepreneurs, succession is not primarily about money. It is about finding the person who can serve her clients as she has and keep the team in place. According to Betty, "I am actively looking. We have significant life insurance to protect our family, but [I fear] an unexpected disability or demise would leave things very confused."

## LISA SAPPENFIELD BOYER
### CFP®, REGISTERED PRINCIPAL, INVESTMENT ADVISOR REPRESENTATIVE, BOYER AND SAPPENFIELD INVESTMENT ADVISORS, TRANSAMERICA FINANCIAL ADVISORS

> I am blessed to have a thirty-year-old son who has worked for me since he graduated college at age twenty-two. He would say he has been working for me since he was ten or younger. He is such a blessing for me and my clients. I am currently out of the office one week a month (my thirty-year goal) for conferences and time off.

Lisa says she plans to work at least another fifteen years, so she is early in her succession planning. She says that the biggest challenge she and her son will have in the next few years is finding a replacement for her long-time office manager when she retires. "I am not sure they make people like her anymore." Another challenge will be finding a business partner for her son to help him handle all the business when she is no longer working.

Lisa and her son have a buyout agreement for either disability or death. She credits her broker-dealer with providing them with the information and resources to allow this to happen. Her broker-dealer also does the valuation of the business with a formula included in the buyout agreement. Because Lisa's successor is likely to be her son, she has discounted the final number by 15 percent. ("I can't give others that discount.) She is also pleased about the valuable input her son was able to provide as they completed the agreement in order to ensure he could keep the staff, pay off the business, and pay himself.

Like many in the financial services profession, Lisa and her husband have taken her own financial planning advice and invested over the years. These investments would allow her to retire at her current age of fifty-three if she chose. But like all of the women in this study, she loves what she does and has no plans to retire in the near future. Her husband has assured her that he will not need the proceeds of the business sale if something were to happen to her or if she were to retire. However, her son is adamant, according to Lisa, that he will purchase the business. He sees the money from the sale going to his brother and sister one day.

Lisa says that she and her son work well together "because he is really laid back like his dad and not hyper like his mother. I have heard horror stories about the parents who won't work but won't stay out of running the business. When we decide it is his, then his it will be. He can ask for advice and help when he wants. I also know to be successful, it will have to be different and continue to change!"

## MELANIE, SHANTY
## CRPC®, R.S.S. FINANCIAL SERVICES, INC., LINCOLN FINANCIAL ADVISORS

For Melanie and her son, succession planning has been a large part of their partnership. She was in her fifties when she and Jason started working together. "Our goal has always been for him to take over the business in a ten-year period." They have hired a professional coach who is an expert in succession planning and has helped countless advisors build succession plans. "As a woman and Jason's mom, I knew that we would need a lot of assistance in charting this new path."

Melanie sees herself as continuing to be involved in the practice, "albeit playing a much smaller background role." She also reports that her broker-dealer has begun a new rigorous succession planning effort because of all of the advisors who are approaching retirement age. She and Jason plan to take full advantage of this new project.

Melanie Shanty (second from left) and her three children.

## PAMELA GILMOUR
### CPA, CFP®, CLU, CHFC, CASL, FINANCIAL PLANNER AND OWNER, FINANCIAL FITNESS, GUARDIAN LIFE INSURANCE COMPANY OF AMERICA

Although Pamela still has at least five years before retirement, she hopes her current business model will become her succession plan. She has two young male employees who are fully licensed. One of them is present at every client meeting, whether in person or using remote technology. Her office is paperless, and each client has her or his own website "where account balances are updated daily and all financial data is housed."

One of the employees handles all client annual reviews; the other sits in on all new client meetings. They each bring a few of their own new clients into the practice each year. They run the office, and Pamela continues to bring in new clients. She works to help her employees learn the business and continue to "self-improve." Toward this end, each of them does all the analysis for each case, makes recommendations, and discusses them with her. She presents the recommendations to the clients. Both of them have worked with Pamela for more than four years. They are salaried and receive bonuses. All her clients have met them and are comfortable working with them. While she has not spoken directly to her clients about her retirement, they are aware that her two employees will be involved in servicing her accounts in the future. She currently has business overhead insurance and personal disability insurance, which could keep the firm running for two years. In the event of her death, term life insurance benefits would pay her employees during a transitional period. However, she does not yet have a written plan for how her clients would be serviced in the event of a disaster. Preparing this written plan is her goal for first quarter 2015.

"My intent is to have these two employees continue in the business with one being the owner." However, according to Pamela, they are young and lack life exposure, which translates into confidence. She says of her most likely successor:

> He has yet to take on full sales responsibility ... eating what he kills ... and is not interested in the insurance agency field representative model ... While he could assume my investment fees and trails, my insurance renewals would not be available to him. It will be critical that he can add thirty plus clients a year to my base in order for him to be profitable.

Pamela, like most of the other women with insurance practices, says that her "mother insurance company" has nothing in place to help with succession. "The ideal situation would be to sell my [insurance] practice to another ... agent in this area, who runs a practice like mine." She is currently researching outside companies to value her investment practice, make it more saleable, and possibly connect her with potential buyers.

# KAREN DEROSE
## CFP®, CRPC®, MANAGING PARTNER, DEROSE FINANCIAL PLANNING GROUP, LINCOLN FINANCIAL ADVISORS

Karen, like Melanie and Lisa, has a son who has joined her in the business. She also has a female employee who began working for her right out of college with a business degree and personal finance concentration. Karen hopes that she will become her second successor. This young woman is the financial planning manager of Karen's practice, knows the planning process and software, and manages all clients' plans with the help of her broker-dealer planning department.

Karen has attempted to partner with junior associates and believes she has a better understanding of the kind of people who will fit into her practice. She has worked with new associates using the industry model of requiring them to "go out and hunt and bring in new business with some guidance." However, this model has not produced positive results. Therefore, Karen has reverted to how her father successfully trained her. For her first three years in the business, Karen went on appointments with him and watched him sell. Observing him taught her products, how to follow up, and processes. Since the hunt-and-eat-what-you-kill approach to training failed with previous associates, she decided to have her son attend all her client appointments for a period of time to help him build his knowledge and confidence.

Although her son decided to join her in the business sooner than they had previously agreed upon, the timing turned out to be right. She says that her business was at a crossroads. It had become too large for her to handle. So she had to either stop taking on new clients or "embrace him joining" her practice as she continues to grow it.

The first year, she paid her son the same salary he was earning with his previous employer: $66,000. She did this because he had multiple appropriate degrees and because she did not want him to have to move back home. His second year, she did a lot of soul-searching and decided that she would make him a 10 percent partner in the business instead of paying him for new clients, which is a model that has worked for some. Making him a minority partner is working very well. He is learning how to grow the business and maintain the company culture of creating a great client-practice experience. He is a stakeholder in the business with all clients.

Karen is now thinking about how best to incorporate the female financial planning manager when she is ready to become a financial planner. Karen, like all of the women in this study, wants to be fair to a valued team member who has been a dedicated employee with a passion for the business. She recognizes that two people will need to run her practice, so there is ample room for both her son and the financial planning manager. If either her son or the financial planning manager is not successful as a partner, she will try again to partner with another young financial planner.

Karen DeRose (right) diving with her two sons. She says
that she dives every year, but it still terrifies her.

Karen is working on a valuation of her business and believes it would be fairly easy to sell due to her three income streams: fees, assets under management, and insurance. She and her son have a buyout agreement that they review and sign each year. Her broker-dealer has offered seminars to help with succession planning but is only now developing a larger initiative.

She concurs with most of the other women featured in this book. Lack of good succession plans for retiring financial services professionals is a major problem for the industry. So many successful professional financial planners are rapidly reaching retirement age, and so few highly motivated young professionals are waiting to take their places. Karen echoes what other successful women in this study have said, "What really concerns me is that my clients and staff are well cared for."

## NANCY WOLFE-SMITH
### CLU, FLMI, LUTCF, MBA, NANCY WOLFE-SMITH INSURANCE AGENCY, INC., STATE FARM

Nancy Wolfe-Smith plans to retire. However, she cannot sell her agency; it reverts back to the company when she retires. So that this does not happen, she is mentoring one of her young team members who aspires to be an agent and have her own agency. "I'm constantly preparing her by sharing challenges and how to overcome them. I'm open and honest with her about everything. I've also given her responsibilities and regularly ask for her ideas and opinions."

Nancy is trying to help this young woman "think like a business owner." Her goal is to have this young woman put her name on the door when Nancy retires. Once she retires, Nancy says she will always be available to be a mentor.

## DOING THE WORK I LOVE FOR AS LONG AS POSSIBLE IS THE PLAN FOR SOME

Other women featured in this book plan to work as long as possible and do not have specific retirement dates in mind. Most of these women are already taking advantage of more time away from the office, which is made possible by the successful business and teams they have worked so hard to build. As what her company calls a "national resource" in the areas of estate and business planning, Dianna Parker does not have a specific succession plan. Since her clients all have another financial planner who has referred them to her, she does not have the same level of concern about making sure all of her clients are well served; she knows they will be.

Anne Machesky believes that there are "not a lot of great solutions for older advisors." She says that most of the older advisors "do not see an exit door." She, like most of her contemporaries in the financial services profession, loves what she does. Since older advisors are "young of mind," they plan to stay in the game. She doesn't believe that the industry has done a very good job of helping older financial professionals develop a succession or exit plans. She says it is talked about at company meetings all the time, but no "runways" are offered. Likewise, she is not optimistic about finding young professionals to replace the successful professionals who practice today. "There are few behind us who appear to have the strong mix of work ethic, long-term commitment, idealism about people and institutions, and the patience to care for the dynamic between finances and human goals."

Anne Machesky (center) and her family.

Retirement, succession, and business continuation are the most difficult business transitions most of these women will experience. Even those who will not have their own succession plans because they do not own their clients will find that turning client files over to their companies or agencies is far more difficult because of the promises and commitments they have made to these clients over the years.

Some of these women may find it difficult to exit the business; as Anne Machesky suggests, they may be emotionally unable to retire. Many will look for the middle ground, such as finding a successor partner with whom to work for some years after traditional retirement age, enabling her to limit her time in the business while ensuring her clients are being served. Others will find that finding the perfect successor to service her clients, maintain her team, and purchase her business is exceedingly difficult and may have to compromise.

The lucky ones will find that successor, will mentor her or him as she moves toward limiting her time and involvement in the business. The successor will enjoy working with her and learning from the joint work they do with her clients. Although she will be missed by her clients and her team, she knows her successor and the team will take care of them.

# CHAPTER 9

# A ROADMAP TO SUCCESS FOR FINANCIAL SERVICES PROFESSIONALS

> Persevere. This is not an easy business to learn, not an easy business to begin, not an easy business to build, and certainly it's still a *man's world*. But I believe that women have something unique and special to offer in this profession, and would love to see more women entering.
>
> —Dianna Parker, CFP®, National Resource, Sagemark Consulting, Lincoln Financial Advisors
>
> Find your passion. When you are passionate about what you do, it is no longer work.
>
> —Gail Linn, CFP®, CASL, ChFC, LUTCF, Financial Services Representative, Financial Planner, MetLife Premier Client Group of NYC

Dianna Parker on the road in Mykonos, Greece.

## A ROADMAP TO SUCCESS: DEFINED

Although each very successful woman in the financial services industry defines her business success differently, she has achieved this success with values and business practices that are congruent with those of the other successful women in the profession. Of course, there are differences in the paths they have taken, but all the successful women interviewed for this book agree on what needs to be done if one is to be successful in a financial services career. This chapter will lay out a roadmap of steps that are likely to add up to a very successful, fulfilling career for women in the financial services industry.

You can begin your journey on this roadmap (and in the career) in different places, depending upon whether you have just decided that financial services is a career you want to pursue or you have already been in the career for a number of years. The roadmap will suggest variations of how you can accomplish the same goals if you are single and live at home with your parents or are a married or suddenly single woman with children.

While you travel along this roadmap, be sure to pause for a refreshing bit of wisdom from the amazingly successful women you have come to know as you have read this book. Some of their words of advice were given in response to the question: "What advice would you give your daughter or niece if she were entering the business?" However, you will also find golden nuggets that simply come from these women reflecting on their experiences in this career and in their lives. We hope you will use this roadmap to plan the steps you will take to become as successful as these women who have been so willing to share their careers with you.

## EDUCATION PRIOR TO ENTERING THE CAREER

- A college degree is the educational foundation for a financial services career.
- Majoring in finance, business, economics, or sales will give you a head start.
- If you do not major in a related field, take as many electives as possible in those fields.
- A solid fundamental background in mathematics is important.
- Part-time or summer jobs in the financial services industry can provide you with a picture of what to expect.
- An internship (paid or unpaid) with a financial services company may give you the opportunity to learn about the company, products, sales, and the career.
- Seek professional designations, such as CFP®, while still in college. Many colleges and universities offer courses leading to professional designations.
- Join campus organizations of women (and men) seeking financial services careers. Attend local (WIFS or NAIFA chapter) and/or national professional meetings in the field whenever possible. Many professional organizations have opportunities and inexpensive dues for college students.
- Check the websites of professional organizations (website addresses are listed in Appendix D).

## ADVICE FROM SUCCESSFUL WOMEN

Get as much education as possible as soon as possible. The more knowledge you have about finance and the career, the better equipped you will be to weather the first few difficult years. Take advantage of every opportunity to learn about and experience the career. Do your research. Search the Internet for financial services offices, agencies, or companies near your college, university, or home. Call them and tell them you would be interested in a part-time or full-time position while in school. Or pursue a summer job with them. Be willing to do anything. And as Robelynn Abadie says, "Be a sponge." Internet research can also help you determine which financial services companies offer internships. Are there any in your area? Are they summer or school-year internships? Are they available following graduation? How do you apply?

If you have already graduated from college with a totally unrelated degree or didn't finish your degree, consider the following:

- Many financial services companies require a college degree as a prerequisite to begin a career as an agent, financial representative, financial planner, wealth manager, or other professional career-track positions. Some do not.
- If you do not already have a degree, consider taking courses in a field related to your chosen career. Many colleges and universities offer professional degree-track programs in the evenings, on weekends, or online (*distance learning*).
- While pursuing your degree, a *paying* job in a local financial services agency or company can provide you with practical knowledge of the profession, a means of applying what you are learning in your courses, and experience that will help you obtain an appropriate job when you finish your degree.
- If you already have completed an undergraduate degree in an unrelated field, a graduate degree in finance, insurance, business, or a related field might make sense. Again, a search of the Internet will help you find colleges and universities with appropriate degrees; many have evening or online programs for students who are working.

- If you are working in another field and cannot go back to school, you can pursue licensing on your own, take courses, or do self-study for a professional designation. You might also want to look at distance-learning opportunities offered by accredited institutions.

- Use the Internet to locate financial services businesses in your community. Attempt to determine the best person to call to set an appointment to discuss a possible paid position in the office, agency, or company. Put together a good résumé and interview this person about a job in his or her business. Be sure to tell him or her that you are interested in a career as a financial representative, agent, financial planner, wealth manager (find the appropriate title on their website and use the correct term in the interview). Mention that you want to have the opportunity to learn more about the business before you jump in. Ask if there is a position in the agency or with one of the agents where you could work for a few years to experience the business and gain an education. Be sure to interview more than one business.

- Of course, you can also jump in, which we will discuss more in depth in the next section.

> I have a master's degree in music from Southern Methodist University and a CFP® designation. I was a career changer when I joined the firm as a Reregistered Representative. You might not think a degree in music would be very helpful in this profession, but actually it has been. I have found my training and experience as a performer on stage to be very beneficial in the work I do today. When you study any field at a high level, you are not only increasing your knowledge in that field, but you are learning how to learn and how to leverage resources. This, too, has been invaluable to me in my financial services career.
>
> —Dianna Parker

## FINDING THE BEST PLACE TO BEGIN YOUR FINANCIAL SERVICES CAREER

One of the wonderful things about the financial services profession is that you can practice it almost anywhere in the United States, Canada, and many other countries as long as there are people who need financial advice. The women interviewed for this book live in major cities, small cities, suburbs, and rural areas. You can work completely independently, like Kathleen Godfrey, be a captive agent of a single company, or have your own company and utilize the products and services of a broker-dealer and one or more insurance companies.

Anne Machesky says, "The field is an open landscape of opportunity for helping clients, colleagues, [and] management, and it is in constant change. You create your opportunities and process by applying your values and passions in the service of others."

## WITH ALL THE OPPORTUNITIES, HOW DO YOU FIND THE BEST PLACE TO BEGIN?

- Know your passion.
- Be true to yourself.
- Who do you want to help?
- Are there particular products and services you want to deliver?
- What kinds of people are you most comfortable being with and working with?
- What personal experiences have led you to your decision to pursue a financial services career?
- What kind of a work environment is most comfortable to you?
- How do you learn?

> Be yourself. Women are uniquely qualified for this business with a high level of empathy and care. We are good listeners. We are jugglers.
>
> —Betty Harris Custer

- Careers in the financial services industry outside of the corporate environment are primarily entrepreneurial. This means that you are beginning your own business and you will be paying your own salary and benefits (and over time, the salaries and benefits of your team and staff) from the work you generate and quality of the advice you give and services you provide. If you are *not* comfortable with this, consider taking a paid position in the industry.

- Research and analysis is a key to finding the best place for you in the industry. Fortunately, research today is simplified by *careful* use of the Internet.
- What companies, agencies, or offices are within a reasonable commute from where you live or hope to live?
- Are there companies, agencies, or offices in a community where you know many people and many people know you? Is this a better place to begin a career in which referrals are the most effective way to build a clientele?
- If living in a community where you have previously lived is not an option, are you comfortable networking and cold calling to meet prospective clients?
- How do the independent financial rating services rate the companies in the community where you plan to begin your career? (Check the following for ratings of all financial services companies: Fitch, Moody's, Standard and Poor's, and A. M. Best [insurance], Weiss [banks and insurance].)
- What do the agency's or company's clients say about the product they have purchased and the services they have received? (Be a thoughtful consumer of all information obtained online.)
- Is the company's primary business insurance, investments, financial planning, banking, or a combination of the above? Does the company focus on one aspect of the business more than another?
- What type of products does it sell or recommend?

Make a list of those companies, offices, or agencies you would like to interview. Call and make an appointment to meet with the highest-ranking person in the office. You are also interviewing him or her while he or she is interviewing you. If your only option is to meet with a recruiter or a member of the human resources staff, you may want to pursue the interview and attempt to schedule a subsequent interview with a financial services professional in the office. Be sure the person answering the phone knows you are interviewing him or her to determine whether you are interested in pursuing a career with their company.

- Decide what you want the outcome of your interview to be.
- Meet female financial services professionals in the office.
- Meet with the office principal, manager, owner, or general agent.
- Schedule a second interview.
- Tour the office.
- Learn how financial professionals are compensated.
- Learn about the training program, education offered, and expectations.

Prepare the questions you will ask in advance. Base the questions on what you have learned about the company on the website. Be sure to use correct terminology to refer to the professionals in the office and the type of business they do. Ask questions about the business that will be important to your decision-making process (i.e., How many women financial planners work in this office?). Asking difficult questions reveals who you are and what is important to you (i.e., I have two young children, and I will not be able to attend meetings prior to eight thirty or after five o'clock; will this be a problem? I need to earn at least _____ per year to meet my financial obligations; can I do this in my first year in the business?). If the answers to these questions are not helpful, keep looking for a manager in a financial services agency, office, or company who will work with you to meet your personal and professional needs.

- Make a good first impression. Wear conservative business attire, be on time, practice a firm handshake, smile, hand the person you are interviewing an updated résumé, ask clear prepared questions, take notes and ask permission to do so, and be polite and friendly. Never fail to show up for an interview you have scheduled. If for some reason you are delayed or must reschedule, call immediately and apologize directly to the person you have inconvenienced.

- As soon as possible after the interview, jot down notes about the person you interviewed, your impressions of the office, additional questions you would like to ask in a subsequent interview, names of people you want to meet in the office, etc.
- Send a thank-you letter to the person you interviewed and anyone else you met during your visit who gave of their time on your behalf. If you previously established next steps, reiterate them. If not, make clear what you would like the next steps to be.
- Interview as many companies as possible in the open landscape of the financial services industry.
- At the end of the process, ask yourself:
  - Which company or companies do business in a way that matches my values, skills, and interests?
  - Do the companies have policies and procedures that meet my needs?
  - What agencies, offices, or companies have managers who will accommodate my needs and help me reach my goals?
  - Am I comfortable with the training and education I will receive?
  - Can I meet the company's expectations?
  - Do I like the feel of the office? Is it a happy, safe, comfortable environment?
  - Do the values of the professionals to whom I spoke fit my values?
  - If the position is commission or fees only, can I support myself for up to a year without any real income?

---

If I had been in an agency that didn't support women and motherhood and all that that encompasses, I would not have had the success I've had. I was able to work smart while my children were in school, never working evenings or weekends. I developed a practice among professionals because I had to adhere to a daytime schedule and could only meet with successful people who had the freedom to meet with me during the day.

—Ginger Weiss

---

- Select the company (companies) where you want to interview for a professional position. The process is likely to involve taking several tests to determine whether you are a good fit for the business and the way they work. It may also include meeting with several different people and attending meetings to help determine whether the position is right for you. If you decide to pursue a career (or a job) with the company, you will need to get contracted with the company, be fingerprinted, go through a background check, and take more tests. If you have not already done so, you will need to get licensed. Expect this process to take from several weeks to more than a few months.

- Make sure your family is on board and supportive of your decision to become a financial services professional. Educate them about what they can expect with you in the career. Be sure they understand how you will be compensated. Suggest that they meet with the manager or another professional in the agency, office, or company where you plan to begin your career.

> First and foremost, my parents were a huge influence on my career and my drive to succeed. They were living examples that anything is possible if you work hard enough and stay true to yourself. As I started in the business, they were huge supporters. My husband has always supported me and still does. Even to this day, when I'm in a funk, he always seems to get me to see the light at the end of the tunnel.
>
> —Nicole Holland-Hong

## GETTING STARTED AS AN ENTREPRENEUR IN THE FINANCIAL SERVICES INDUSTRY: STAY THE COURSE

Over and over, the women responding to the 2012 WIFS survey and those interviewed for this book talk about how difficult the first three to five years were in the business, how many times they thought about quitting, and how glad they are that they stayed the course. In chapter 2, we discussed those early years and many of the reasons why so many women (and men) leave the industry before they really know how wonderful the career can be. If you want to have the flexibility, satisfaction, and income the industry affords, you need to work very hard in the early years to gain the knowledge you will need, build your clientele, learn how to give advice and close business, build a sales and a service team, and become confident and comfortable in what you do. The successful women featured in this book provide direct advice and relate personal experiences that can help you make these early years happier and more productive.

> Be prepared to work *really* hard for at least three to four years. No matter how hard it seems, don't give up—success is yours if you just stay with it. Find and nurture an inner circle of trustworthy colleagues and friends who will lift you up and keep you in the game.
>
> —Kathleen Godfrey

## THE EARLY YEARS ARE AN ON-THE-JOB EDUCATION

Think of the first three to five years in the business as an advanced education in finance and entrepreneurship. Remember that many professions (i.e., medicine and law) require years of education prior to starting in the career. The financial services industry does not have specific entry-level education requirements. However, the first years in the business are the educational proving ground of the profession. The good news for you is that you can learn and gain experience while you are earning an income. Your income may be very modest in the beginning, but you will not pay tuition. And usually within nine months, you are getting a regular check—sometimes sooner if the company you join has a small salary while you are learning.

Gaining knowledge as soon as possible is important to early success and confidence. If you have come into the industry with a degree in a related field, a professional designation, work experience in the industry, and appropriate licenses, you have a leg up. However, do not despair if you do not have these since there are many ways you can make the process of gaining knowledge quicker and more enjoyable.

> This is a business that requires a lot of upfront work, continual learning not only in the financial area but in relationships, with complexities and challenges abounding.
>
> —Colleen Bowler

Introduce yourself to the most successful and positive people in the office. (Actually, introduce yourself to everyone in the office.) However, ask the positive, successful professionals if you can bring a cup of coffee to them one morning or a glass of iced tea one afternoon and spend fifteen minutes learning about them. Simply ask them to give you their best advice for getting started in the business because you plan to be as successful as they are. Most of them will have lots of advice to give, and you will need to remind them when the fifteen minutes is up.

Find a mentor, preferably a woman. Perhaps one of the successful professionals you met with will simply take on the task of mentoring you. You might ask one or more of them if you can meet with them for a short time each week.

> Find a mentor and follow! Be willing to listen and learn. Be grateful that someone has taken an interest in you.
>
> —Colleen Bowler

If you do not find an appropriate mentor in your office, ask your manager or trainer if she or he knows of someone in your region who might be interested in helping you learn the business. Check with your company or broker-dealer. Ask if they have a mentoring program.

Do joint work. Introduce your prospects and clients to successful professionals in your agency who have skills and knowledge that you do not yet possess. Develop strategic partnerships with colleagues and other professionals (i.e., attorneys, CPAs, insurance professionals, and investment specialists).

> Surround yourself with successful people who will influence you and be a positive reflection on you, even if you don't have all of the answers yourself.
>
> —Barbara Brazda Dietze

Join a professional organization, particularly one with local presence. WIFS and NAIFA often have local chapters. If WIFS does not have a local chapter, check their website to learn how to join, participate in monthly webinars, and find a WIFS mentor.

Attend professional meetings in your community, and as soon as possible, attend a national professional meeting. Ask the successful professionals you interviewed if they attend any professional meetings—and if they would be willing to have you join them and be introduced to the group.

If you have not yet found a mentor, perhaps you will find one in a local chapter of a national professional organization. Volunteer to get involved in the activities of the chapter.

Attend meetings sponsored by your company. Go to the meetings expecting to learn a lot, be inspired, and meet many of the most successful people in your company. Know who you want to meet before attending the meeting. Prepare questions you want to ask those professionals. While being respectful of their time, introduce yourself and ask if you might ask them a question. If they are approachable, ask if they might have time to have a brief phone conversation with you.

Explore the education and training section of your company's or broker-dealer's website. Learn what programs are available and how you sign up to participate in them. Check to see if your company or broker-dealer has female study groups for new financial professionals. Get involved with a study group of other new female financial services professionals.

Sign up to begin a professional education or designation program. For many of the women interviewed for this book, particularly those who began their careers in large insurance companies, LUTCF sponsored by NAIFA was a good choice. The courses you take for this designation provide technical information and practical information about how to sell, develop a clientele, and run a business. Some companies will help you pay for courses and designations from organizations, such as NAIFA, the American College (i.e., CLU, ChFC, etc.) or CFP®. Check with your trainer, manager, or company to determine what is recommended and available.

Pursue all licenses as quickly as possible. Most companies or broker-dealers will provide you with information about which to pursue first. And many companies or broker-dealers will pay for them.

## WORKING HARD AND WORKING SMART ARE CRITICAL AT THE START

Starting in the business when you are young, single, and without children can be a significant advantage because it allows you the freedom and time to get through the difficult early years before you add responsibilities. If you can live at home with supportive parents, you may also remove some of the financial stress of little or no income for several months.

If you are starting the career married or single with children, be sure that you have made adequate arrangements for the care of the children during the day while you are at work. Is your husband or significant other supportive of your decision to become a successful entrepreneur? Is he willing to pinch-hit when you cannot prepare dinner or pick up the children at school? Is your manager supportive of parenthood and will he or she work with you to become successful even if you cannot attend early-morning meetings or after-hours training sessions?

> I did have a manager/mentor . . . who continues to be a role model for me today. When I was frantic or tearful, he had a way of pulling me out of the trees so that I could see the forest ... He is also a fine husband and father. I had a two-year-old and four-month-old when I joined this profession. [He] once told me, on a day when I was fearful of rescheduling some client meetings because of a sick child, that "[your children] are only on loan to you." This is something I will never forget, and I have passed it along to many of my colleagues and friends who were feeling guilty or struggling with the *right* balance of career and family.
>
> —Dianna Parker

Hire staff as soon as possible. Many of the successful women in the WIFS study hired staff, often shared with another professional, in their first year in the business. Twenty-two of the twenty-three women featured in the book had a least one full-time staff member by her third year in the business.

- Is there a stipend available for helping you pay for staffing?
- Does your company or broker-dealer provide you with information about how to select, hire, compensate, and train staff?
- Is there someone else in your office with similar values and work ethic with whom you could share an employee?

Get organized. Develop systems. Become a good manager of your time. Think highest and best use of your time and talent for yourself and for your team members. Develop a business plan. Set clear, achievable goals that will move you to the next level of your business. For the most successful women in the WIFS survey and featured in this book, achieving the goals they set for themselves was their biggest motivator. Many offices, agencies, and companies have sample business plans you can use. Include such things as the following:

- production goals
- client attainment goals
- education goals (i.e., I will complete three courses toward my CFP® by December _____.)
- "minimum acceptable" case size or client goals (i.e., My "minimum acceptable client" has a family annual income of $200,000.)
- acceptable client practice goals (i.e., My clients will respond to all communications within _____.)
- staffing goals
- recognition and achievement goals (i.e., I will achieve MDRT status by December _____ or I will be in the top five hundred producers in my broker-dealer by _____.)
- other professional goals (i.e., I will attend the NAIFA national meeting in _____.)

The successful women featured in this book ask no more of their clients than they do themselves. They value their team members and colleagues, women and men, and treat them with kindness and respect. Adopt the same principles for yourself.

> Manage your finances and always save from every check. Walk the talk. Inspire other women to be financially secure and smart.
>
> —Pamela Gilmour

- be a model for your clients
- have your own financial plan
- take your own advice
- do what you advise them to do

> Women can be the worst enemies of other women. There have rarely been men who have crossed this divide . . . It's been there, just because it can be a very competitive environment. But many women are mean-spirited and not able to talk things out or through. [Women often lack] the ability to take a step back and recognize someone for their efforts.
>
> —Robelynn Abadie

- join a study group
- be as supportive of other women as you expect them to be of you

Keep all lines of communication open with your manager(s). Do not complain, but also do not hesitate to tell your manager what help you need in order to be successful. Be cautious not to complain to your colleagues or staff about management or office practices and procedures. If these are more than small annoyances and are interfering with your progress, discuss your concerns without rancor with the people who can actually remedy them.

Laugh and cry with your colleagues. Work hard—but have fun.

> Work hard. Believe that the right clients will show up for you to serve. Be trustworthy, stay ethical and caring, and never give up on yourself.
>
> —Anne Machesky

## GROWING YOUR PRACTICE: SUCCESS

Every woman featured in this book loves the work she does. She is fulfilled by helping her clients and their families achieve their financial goals. She respects the company or broker-dealer with whom she is affiliated and appreciates all the good services and products they provide to her and her clients. She has worked diligently to put together a team of professionals who allow her to do what she does best: work directly with her clients. She works in an environment that is safe, productive, friendly, and happy. She lives the life she wants to lead: is home with her family often, is always busy but works fewer hours than in years past, is good to herself, takes vacations, gives of her time to others, and participates in activities she loves. She is successful in the ways she chooses to succeed and far more so than she ever anticipated.

How did these women get to this point in their careers? For almost all of them, the early years were difficult. Juggling children, work, sometimes spouses, volunteer service, and other random activities often left her exhausted. She frequently felt alone, and at times, she lacked the support of her managers, colleagues, spouse, and friends. For those who had the support of family, friends, mentors, and managers, the difficult years were far less stressful, but they were never easy.

These women achieved the success and the good lives they have today through hard work, perseverance, integrity, belief in themselves, selflessness, and a passion for the importance of the work they do for others.

> After the initial years, decide who you want to be in this amazing business. Then, do all you can to get there.
>
> —Robelynn Abadie

# YOU CAN'T GET TO WHERE YOU ARE GOING UNLESS YOU KNOW WHERE IT IS

Plan for today, plan for this year, and plan for the future. Have a detailed business plan. Have a vision for your business. Know your mission—and be able to communicate it. Include the core values of your business in your plan. Have measurable goals and objectives to help you achieve those goals. Be sure that your team members are included in your plan and participate in your planning process.

> From the business plan of Nancy Wolfe-Smith:
>
> My team members and I are dedicated to positive, ethical, and caring interaction with our clients and each other. We are committed to building our knowledge base, taking on new challenges with optimism, and growing the business. We meet daily, weekly, monthly, and quarterly to ensure that we are working together toward the same goals. We work as one to help our clients.

Develop a marketing plan. How will you service existing clients? How will you grow your business with new clients? What is your brand—and how does it distinguish you from others? What marketing materials do you need to develop? What process must you go through to get them approved? What networks do you need to join? Who on your team can help?

> From the business plan of Colleen Bowler:
>
> We are dedicated to helping our clients "get all the way home."

Reconfigure your staff to be congruent with your business plan. Do they have—or can they gain—the knowledge and skills you need to help you grow your business? Are they good team players? Do they work well with you, each other, and your clients? What new roles will each of them play? Do not hesitate to remove staff members who do not fit in with your business plan or are not helping you grow.

From the business plan of Nancy Wolfe-Smith:

We work well with others. We believe that to succeed, we need positive partnerships with both operations and other agents. My team members have helped to train other agents' team members in areas where we are successful. We have shared our client engagement ideas with agents across the company because we know that for our agency system to succeed, every agent needs to be successful.

Staff up. Do you need to add additional staff? Do you need to replace staff? Make your staff a team. Empower your team members—and then let them do what they do well.

I am leader of my team every day.

—Toni Espey

I hope to keep my team together as long as possible.

—Lisa Sappenfield Boyer

Toni Espey (right) and her mom who has been an important member of her team since the beginning.

## EVERYONE NEEDS PROFESSIONAL HELP

- Hire a coach.
- Search for a coach who can provide you with the assistance you need to develop and implement your business and marketing plans.
- Talk to your successful colleagues. *Do you have a coach? Who? Why did you pick him or her? What does she or he do best? Would you recommend her or him for me?*
- If appropriate, ask for a referral.
- Call and interview the coach.
- Check with your professional organizations to see if they endorse any coaches or have any who offer a discount to members.
- Check with your company or broker-dealer. Do they have any coaches to recommend or any whose fee they will subsidize? (If you go this route, be sure the coach will be working for you—and not for the company or your manager.)
- Check the website of the coach. Does it appear from the website that the coach can help you in the areas where you most need assistance?
- Ask for references and call them.

> All of us should have coaches.
>
> —Colleen Bowler

Consider hiring other coaches or consultants to help implement short-term goals:

- developing a client-friendly website
- leveraging your social media and Internet presence
- establishing and communicating your brand
- working on public relations and marketing
- conducting personality and skill assessments of your current staff
- hiring new staff

Colleen Bowler with her husband and "the big fish."

Pamela Gilmour: Sometimes you may need to look at things upside down.

Join a new study group of some of the most successful professionals in the industry. Become immediately active in the group. Volunteer for the grunt work that keeps the study group together.

Pursue leadership positions in professional organizations. Network with the most successful professionals in the industry—not just your company or broker-dealer. Attend all company, broker-dealer, and professional organization events that put you in contact with professionals who have achieved what you are working toward.

## YOUR WORK ENVIRONMENT MAY BE IMPORTANT TO THE IMPLEMENTATION OF YOUR BUSINESS PLAN

Change, remodel, redecorate, and improve your work environment. Consider changing offices if necessary. Many of the women in this study said they could have been successful more quickly if they had moved out of their corporate or agency offices sooner. If that is not an option, consider doing more work from home. Tell your manager what you need in order to make your office comfortable for growing your business. Ask for help. Consider the following:

- Is your environment comfortable for meeting with clients?
- Do you have a comfortable, private space to meet with your clients?
- Are your team members able to work productively and in private?
- Do you have all of the technology you need to reach your business goals and serve your clients? If not, is it available through your company or broker-dealer? Do you need to purchase it from an outside source? If you purchase technology from an outside source, be sure to check with your company or broker-dealer to be sure it is compliant and compatible with company software.
- Are your office and the offices of your team members comfortable, welcoming, safe, and pleasant?
- Is parking convenient for you, your staff, and your clients?
- Is there a comfortable place for clients to wait and work?

From the marketing plan of Karen DeRose:

**Executive Summary**

The first portion of the marketing plan speaks specifically to creating a well thought-out "client experience" with critical leverage points necessary in staying in constant contact with current clients.

## KNOW WHAT YOU WANT YOUR CLIENT'S EXPERIENCE TO BE WITH YOU, YOUR STAFF, AND YOUR COMPANY

- reinvest in your community
- seek membership on boards
- volunteer
- get more involved in things you are passionate about
- encourage or require your team members to become involved

## CONTINUE TO LEARN NEW THINGS

- Seek new professional designations; it is never too late. Consider adding designations that reflect a changing client base (i.e., retirement planning, business succession planning, estate planning, and charitable giving).
- Attend continuing education programs that increase your knowledge of concerns that affect your clients, their businesses, and their families.
- Consider becoming certified and teaching continuing education courses.
- Pursue speaking opportunities with your company, your broker-dealer, professional organizations, senior learning institutes, college and university classes, and your community.
- Consider teaching a class or course at a local college or university. Does the college or university have a chapter of a financial services organization? If yes, could you become an advisor or guest speaker? If not, would it be appropriate for you to work with faculty and students to establish one?
- Network with the professionals in your community who may assist your clients in meeting their changing needs (i.e., estate planning attorneys, trust officers, elder law attorneys, and social security advisors).
- Add to your professional library. Include materials and publications that may help your clients meet their changing needs. Would it be appropriate to have a small, checkout library in your office?

- Consider forming new, more advanced strategic relationships with other professionals.
- Mentor newer financial services professionals, particularly women, while continuing to be mentored yourself by someone who is a model of success for you.

Karen DeRose, never afraid to learn and try new things

## BE TRUE TO YOURSELF: ADVICE FROM SUCCESSFUL WOMEN

- Keep your priorities straight. Your family is always number one! There may be times when it is necessary to step back from your business for the good of your family.

> It is okay for it to take longer in years to achieve a certain status if you are happy with work and family and know how to have fun!
>
> —Lisa Sappenfield Boyer

- Never confuse high income with success. Always put your clients' needs before your profit.

> There have been a few in the business who taught me what not to do: do not make it all about the money; do not sell the highest-priced product. Do not forget your clients have a family at home.
>
> —Colleen Bowler

- Invest in your business and yourself. Don't forget to work on meeting your health and fitness needs.
- Be willing to take carefully considered risks, understanding that it is okay if they do not pan out as expected. Learn from the experience and remember failure is not an option.
- Surround yourself with positive, successful people.
- Commit to helping other women grow in the financial services industry. Pass on your success to others.
- Love your career and the work you do for your clients and others as much as the women interviewed for this book.

The checklist in table 9.1 below provides you with questions based on the success stories of the incredibly successful women you have read about in this book. Ask yourself these questions as you grow your financial services practice. Answering these questions should help you along your road to success.

## FINANCIAL SERVICES CHECKLIST

We've identified key factors to building and maintaining a full, rewarding, and profitable financial services practice and have grouped these into ten distinct areas:

1. Know your passion
2. Service, value, and excellence
3. Education, knowledge, and professionalism
4. Juggling, balance, and blending
5. Role models, mentors, and coaches
6. Business models and plans
7. Hiring staff and building your team
8. Your work environment
9. Transition and succession planning
10. Paying it forward and giving back

Below are questions, grouped under the key factors listed above, for you to consider as you grow your practice.

**KNOW YOUR PASSION**

- ❑ What are my core values?
- ❑ What can I do all day and still have energy?
- ❑ What do others say I am really good at doing?
- ❑ What products/services do I want to deliver?
- ❑ What problems do I want to help people solve?
- ❑ Who do I like being with; what types of people do I work best with and want to help?

## KNOW YOUR PASSION

- ❑ What work environment attracts and motivates me?
- ❑ Do I want to own my own business and be responsible for my own and others income and benefits?
- ❑ Do I want to be on a team or work more independently?

## SERVICE, VALUE, AND EXCELLENCE

- ❑ Do I know what my clients think about the service I deliver?
- ❑ How would my clients describe what I do?
- ❑ Are my service standards written and clear?
- ❑ What products and services do I want to add to my repertoire?
- ❑ Am I ahead of my clients' service expectations?
- ❑ Do I know what type of financial planning is next for each of my clients?
- ❑ Do my clients look forward to our reviews?

## EDUCATION, KNOWLEDGE, AND PROFESSIONALISM

- ❑ What designations do I need or want that are relative to my area of work now and in the future?
- ❑ What help do I need to obtain the desired designations: a tutor, a study partner, or a course?
- ❑ What specialty would I like to be known for?
- ❑ Am I doing joint work effectively and successfully?
- ❑ How do I define professionalism?
- ❑ What does my competition know that I don't know?
- ❑ What do my clients want me to learn so I can serve them better?
- ❑ What do I need to do to get to the next level?

## JUGGLING, BALANCE, AND BLENDING

- ❑ What help do I need at home?
- ❑ What help do I need in the office?
- ❑ What technology will help build efficiencies at work and home?

## JUGGLING, BALANCE, AND BLENDING

- ❏ Who is blowing up my boundaries?
- ❏ Would my home and work calendar be more efficient if I blended them?
- ❏ Do my work team and my family know how to support one another?
- ❏ Are my expectations unrealistic?

## ROLE MODELS, MENTORS, AND COACHES

- ❏ Who is living the life I would like to be living?
- ❏ Whose practice would I like to imitate?
- ❏ Does my company or agency have mentoring or coaching programs or offer subsidies for such?
- ❏ Have I explored MDRT, NAIFA, and WIFS, or other appropriate professional organizations?
- ❏ Can I join a national study group?
- ❏ If I could have any mentor, who would I pick?
- ❏ What strategic partnerships or alliances do I currently have or have an opportunity to establish?
- ❏ Who would I like to do joint work with and why? Who are their ideal clients?
- ❏ Is there someone I can help but haven't reached out to help?

## BUSINESS MODELS AND PLANS

- ❏ Do I have a written business plan?
- ❏ Is it a working, breathing plan or one that sits on the shelf?
- ❏ Am I reviewing and sharing it with anyone?
- ❏ Is my written vision clear?
- ❏ Does my mission align with my vision?
- ❏ Are my goals congruent with my values?
- ❏ What am I tracking and measuring?
- ❏ Do I have clear written strategies?

## BUSINESS MODELS AND PLANS

- ❑ What are the big rocks that need to be moved or removed in my practice?

## HIRING STAFF AND BUILDING YOUR TEAM

- ❑ Do I have the right people on my team? Who is missing?
- ❑ Does my team get the big picture of what I am building?
- ❑ What professional development does my team need?
- ❑ Are my expectations of my team written and clear?
- ❑ Am I leveraging all of my agency's and company's resources?
- ❑ Do I share my plan and goals with my team?
- ❑ Did they help me build my plan? Do they have ownership in the plan?
- ❑ To get to the next level, what adjustments need to be made on my team?
- ❑ Am I focused each day on the highest and best use of my skills and talents?
- ❑ Who can help me with the hiring process? What resources are available to me?

## YOUR WORK ENVIRONMENT

- ❑ Am I energized when I come to my office?
- ❑ What am I tolerating?
- ❑ Is there something I can do to make my office more enjoyable and efficient?
- ❑ Are my clients wowed when they come to my office?
- ❑ Do I feel supported by my team, agency, and company in my work environment?
- ❑ Do I coach people in my office environment how to work best with me?
- ❑ Do I ask for what I want and need? Do I ask the correct person?
- ❑ What would make my environment exciting and fun?

## TRANSITION AND SUCCESSION PLANNING

- ❏ What life triggers are on the horizon?
- ❏ How would having a junior partner or business partner help me grow and transition?
- ❏ Is teaming something I should consider?
- ❏ What additional revenue streams would I like to add to my business?
- ❏ When would I like to step away and retire?
- ❏ What do I need to do to make my business saleable?
- ❏ Who do I know who has gone through a successful transition?
- ❏ What company or agency resources are available to me?

## PAYING IT FORWARD AND GIVING BACK

- ❏ Who made a difference in my journey?
- ❏ Whose journey have I made a difference in?
- ❏ Who within my reach could I help?
- ❏ How am I giving back to my community?
- ❏ What charities and causes do my clients care about?

Table 9.1. *Financial Services Checklist* to help you on your road to success.

# CHAPTER 10 —————————————
# LEARNING FROM AMAZING WOMEN

## AMAZING WOMEN IN THE FINANCIAL SERVICES INDUSTRY

Throughout this book, you have come to know twenty-three of the most successful women in the financial services industry. These women have very different business models. They work with or for many different types of companies. They live in every region of the country, and they do their business in rural areas, suburbs, small cities, and large metropolitan areas. They are married, widowed, divorced, and single, and they have young children, adult children, or no children. What is most striking, however, is what they share.

## SHARED VALUES

All of them are driven by their values. Their families always take precedence over their businesses. When the women are young, their children and spouses come first. As the women mature, their grandchildren, aging parents and in-laws, and other elderly family members and friends consume much of their time and effort.

In their business lives, their decisions are made based on what is in the best interest of their clients. What they earn (which is substantial) and the recognition they are given by their companies and the industry are important to them. However, money and recognition are not important as measures of the women's success. Rather, their status within their companies gives them the opportunity to attend meetings with corporate executives and other significant producers, sharing information and participating in corporate decision making. They also gain access to the best thinkers and advisors within their companies, allowing them to provide their clients with high-level advice and products. Special titles and access to cutting-edge technology and specialized products may also come with their status. Money and recognition make other things possible and come to these women because of the good work they do for their clients. In turn, money and recognition allow them to do more good work for their clients, their families, and their communities.

## PLANNING IS IMPORTANT TO THEIR SUCCESS

All of these women are planners. Many, if not all, are financial planners and advisors. However, even those who are not share in the belief that a values-driven business planning process is critical if they are to succeed. They are organized and develop and adapt processes and procedures as well as goals, objectives, and missions for their practices.

Most of these women have several employees. The work these employees, usually called team members, do is articulated, well thought-out, and important to the successful completion of the business plans that are in place in their practices. Team members are more than assistants to these women; they are highly valued professionals who contribute to the business's success and the advice and service provided to the clients.

## VALUES-DRIVEN SUCCESSION PLANS SUSTAIN THE BUSINESS AND RETAIN TEAM MEMBERS

Not all of the women you met in this book are at the point in their careers where they are developing values-driven succession plans that sustain their businesses and retain their team members so that they can continue providing high levels of advice and service to their clients, even after they have retired. However, they all recognize that if they do not already have a succession plan, they will need one (even those who work for companies where selling the business is not possible).

They also know that developing and implementing a succession plan with the goal of sustaining the business and retaining team members is extraordinarily difficult. As they have done throughout the growth years of their businesses, they will hire coaches and advisors who can help in the valuation of their practices, development of their succession plans, and selection and mentoring of appropriate successors.

They also know that a succession plan that sustains and retains will be more difficult to implement than one that is not committed to the continuation of a values-driven practice. They may partner with numerous potential successors in various roles over a number of years, and they will keep doing so until the fit is right. For these women, succession plans are about more than securing their retirements; they are about making sure their clients continue to receive the advice and service they have come to expect and that their team members continue in a rewarding career path.

## IT TAKES A VILLAGE TO RUN A BUSINESS

These women are team players. Their teams include their employees, business partners, and many other professionals. Most of them have coaches, and many have other professional advisors. They understand and utilize all of the procedures, processes, and products their companies offer. They are active in their companies and the industry. They are mentors and mentees, officers in local and national professional organizations, advocates for women throughout the industry, and important voices for values-driven change in their agencies, offices, companies, and the industry. They are active in their communities and strive to make the lives of all people better with the work that they do.

## THE BLENDED LIFE IS THE COMPLETE LIFE

Although in the early years of their career, these women often found themselves attempting to juggle and balance their personal and business lives. As they established themselves in their businesses, they discovered that there was too much danger that their personal lives or their business lives would suffer if they did not find a way to blend them into one life and become one whole person. For many of these women, their offices became places that welcomed and included children. One room might be turned into a temporary nursery. Team members might become short-term or in-the-moment babysitters. Business trips might also be family vacations. Grandparents might come and go, picking up and dropping off the children of the women and their team members.

Home might also become a workplace. On days when children are ill or not able attend school or day care, technology allows the women and members of their teams to work seamlessly from home. Appointments are sometimes conducted over the phone rather than in person in order to accommodate the family needs of the women, their team members, and their clients.

Technology allows them to conduct staff meetings with team members in remote locations. Even training is done remotely when necessary. These women have whole and complete lives. They have structured their businesses to be inclusive, whenever possible, allowing their lives—and their team members' families and their clients' families—to *intrude* on the workday whenever necessary or desirable.

## KNOWLEDGE AND EDUCATION ARE KEYS TO SUCCESS

These women value education, learning, knowledge, and professionalism. They work hard to gain the knowledge and skills they need to do their jobs at the highest levels. They understand that learning never stops. They seek designations for both the knowledge they gain and the prestige it gives them, their team members, and their businesses.

They expect, encourage, and reward their team members to learn and gain their own designations. They educate their clients. They read, attend professional meetings and seminars, and take courses to increase their knowledge, improve their skills, and provide a rich experience to their team members and clients. They mentor the members of their teams and advance them to positions of responsibility and leadership.

## A CAREER IN FINANCIAL SERVICES IS ENTREPRENEURIAL

These women are entrepreneurs who know how to run successful businesses. Most did not come into the careers with business acumen, but they have gained it through trial, error, hard work, perseverance, and good judgment. Although values drive all their businesses, they know how money flows through a business and how much is needed for salaries, expenses, and growth.

They recognize that business success—and the money that comes from it—allows them to provide robust planning advice, products, and services to their clients. They cannot do this alone, and they cannot do this without understanding the financial ramifications of running a successful business. They seek and hire staff who will help them meet the goals they have for their businesses and clients. They mentor their staff members so they can become professional team members, helping the business grow and serving the clients. They find firing staff members more difficult than hiring them, but they do not hesitate to do so if the staff member is not a positive contributor to business growth and client service. They take calculated risks and do not view those who do not succeed as failures. They persevere. Most of these women are the CEOs and CFOs of their businesses, although some partner with or hire finance professionals to help in this role. They understand that if they are not the leaders of their business, success is not likely.

## GIVING BACK IS NOT OPTIONAL

These women are grateful for all they have been given. They recognize those who have made a large contribution to their lives and businesses: mentors, coaches, family members, managers, colleagues, corporate executives, friends, and a cast of others. And they also know that because they have been given much, it is their responsibility to give back what they have been given to others in their offices, families, communities, companies, and the financial services industry.

They are active participants, serving leadership roles in their companies, professional organizations, and throughout the industry. They are involved in the lives of their children, schools, activities, and churches. If a parent or grandparent is needed, teachers know they can call on these women. They give back physically, emotionally, and financially. And they subtly teach their team members, colleagues, mentees, children, and clients to do the same.

---

## WHAT THESE AMAZING WOMEN HAVE TAUGHT US

Are these women unique? Yes, in many ways they are. However, they are not alone in this uniqueness. Others, women and men, share the same attributes and build incredibly successful, values-driven businesses. What these women have taught us about what they have accomplished and how they have achieved their success—in spite of and because of many challenges along the way—can be replicated.

It is often said that if you attend a conference or a professional meeting and bring one thing of value back to your business the next workday, the meeting was worth attending. We believe this book has given you far more than one thing you can use to change your business and your life. This book, including the roadmap and checklist provided in the previous chapter, gives all in the industry a career lifetime of valuable, practical ideas that can help grow your business into a values-driven, successful practice. You will benefit from what you take away from this book—and so will your employees, team members, families, clients, field managers, companies, and the financial services industry as a whole.

## FINANCIAL SERVICES PROFESSIONALS

Those entering or continuing in entrepreneurial roles in the financial services industry and those beginning or transitioning their businesses can use the lessons learned and taught by these women to help them become their own success stories. And those attempting to find successors who will serve their clients as they have can read what these women have said about finding the best possible successor and sustaining their businesses into the next generation.

No matter where you live or what your current job in the financial services industry, you will gain information from the women featured in this book to grow your practice. Whether you are a recent recruit or a grizzled veteran, you will find golden nuggets of information and advice that can help make your work life more pleasant and rewarding for you, your employees, your families, and your clients. If you read carefully, take to heart the experiences and advice of these women, plan for the future of your business, put together a like-minded team of professionals, and serve your clients well, you will prosper and be able to say, "I love what I do!"

## CORPORATE AND FIELD LEADERS

There is no dispute that women are underrepresented throughout the financial services industry. All financial services companies are seeking women to become financial professionals. The women featured in this book prove that women can be every bit as successful as men.

In addition, women bring traits, skills, and values that are critical in a complex industry that requires ethical and fiduciary responsibility and service. Women build relationships and teams. They and the professional team members they recruit service their clients for a financial lifetime and beyond.

Corporate and field leadership can learn from the WIFS research study that offering a contract to a woman without providing an appropriate infrastructure, excellent education and training, female role models and mentors, flexibility in scheduling meeting and work time, an office that is welcoming, and management and colleagues who believe in and are committed to her success is counterproductive and expensive. However, if these things are in place, women will grow and thrive in the financial services industry. When this occurs, the industry will reach, inform, and serve a much larger percentage of the population than it does today.

All the women in this study are seeking ways, usually through succession plans, to sustain their practices. When corporate and field leadership develop ways to assist the successful women and men in the financial services industry to find and train appropriate successors, everyone will benefit.

## EDUCATORS AND TRAINERS OF FINANCIAL SERVICES RECRUITS AND PROFESSIONALS

The successful women in the WIFS survey and those featured in this book all point to the necessity of early and rigorous education and training. The financial services industry is very complex. Education about finance, products, services, techniques, laws, taxation, ethics, and so much more is critical to the long-term success of professionals in the industry. It is essential that leaders of the industry, educational institutions, and professional organizations come together to find models to educate and train professionals who are expected to provide sophisticated financial advice to individuals, families, businesses, etc.

Many of the women in this study have been in the industry for more than two or three decades. These women and the generation of financial services professionals who are preparing for retirement entered an industry where many companies underwrote and sold a single product.

Representatives from those companies who advised clients and sold life insurance, for example, could easily ask a few questions and scratch out on a single sheet of paper a formula showing how much life insurance the person needed to protect his or her family. Then the only question the client needed to answer was which type of life insurance—term or permanent—was most appropriate.

Life insurance agents who began their careers twenty-five or more years ago saw the career change from selling and servicing a single product to helping clients address a multitude of complex financial questions and delivering a plethora of financial solutions to solve them.

Today, the women in this study—no matter the primary financial discipline of their practices—serve clients who are addressing many questions:

- How do I protect my family if I die or become disabled? Will the money from life and disability insurance be taxed?
- What happens to my financial assets if I declare bankruptcy?

- How will my charitable gifts affect my taxes?
- How do I protect my home, my car, my boat, and other important possessions? What level of liability coverage is needed?
- What is the best way to grow my wealth in a tax-efficient manner? How will this change over time? Who should oversee my investments? What percentage of them need to be liquid?
- What is the best way to save for the education of my children?
- How do I make sure we have enough money for retirement? What are we likely to get from social security and pensions or company retirement funds? Should I maximize my company retirement account? What is the best, most tax-efficient way for me to save for retirement outside of my company account?
- I have a special needs child. How do I make sure that she is cared for if I become disabled or die? How much will her continuing care cost for her lifetime?
- I am getting divorced and have not worked for many years. What do I do now to support my family? How do I get what is rightfully mine? How do I prepare for my retirement?
- My parents need care. What is the best way to finance that care? Will they be able to pay for it?
- How do I make sure that if I—or my spouse—need care in the future, my children do not need to provide the care or pay for it?
- I am planning to retire soon. When would be the best time? Should I take social security now or later? What should my spouse do about her or his social security? Should I annuitize my retirement accounts? When? Should I take a single life payout or some other option?
- How do I make sure that when I die my assets are distributed as I desire?

These questions are only a sampling of the personal finance questions that might be asked of a financial representative, planner, or wealth manager. Every one of these questions has numerous subquestions. If the client owns or is a partner in a business or professional practice, the questions multiply. If the client is the business, the questions involve the family—and how to best provide for employees and succession. Of course, business succession questions become increasingly complex. And none of what appears above considers issues such as the role of technology in the business or how to manage a successful practice. For the most part, the women addressed these issues on their own or with the help of study groups and professional coaches.

It is no longer adequate to expect financial services professionals to acquire all of their professional education and training within a short time on the job. All the women in this study recognize that if they are to grow their businesses to keep up with the increasing complexity of their clients' needs, they must continue their own educations throughout their professional lives—and they have done so.

However, these very successful women also understand that if young financial services recruits are to survive and prosper in the industry they love, they must have a vast amount of knowledge before they meet with a prospect or client. Determining how best to prepare current and future financial services professionals will require the best thinkers in the industry and in education. One of the problems many of the women mentioned in their interviews is that there are too few young financial services professionals prepared to take over the practices of those who came before them.

In addition, these successful women are concerned that if the leadership of the industry does not address how financial services recruits are compensated during their early years in the business, few will enter or remain in the industry. The exponential growth of knowledge and skills required for success and the lack of preservice training and compensation during training are a recipe for disaster. Recruitment and retention have always been problems in the industry, and these women fear that they will become much worse if the great minds in corporations, professional organizations, and educational institutions do not come together to develop an education, training, and apprentice model that rivals those of the medical and legal professions.

From these women, we have learned much. We have learned how they became successful and the joys and pain of achieving that success. What they have accomplished can be replicated.

All the successful women in this study respect and appreciate the good work done by their parent companies. However, they also tell us how very difficult it has been to accomplish what they have achieved. Much of the building of their successful businesses was done on their own with the help of colleagues, team members, and coaches.

These incredibly successful women who care about their clients' futures worry about finding successors who will sustain their practices. Growing a generation of financial services professionals who will be able to sustain the complex and ethical work of the current generation requires the commitment of the entire financial services industry and the organizations and educational institutions that surround it. According to these women, this is imperative—and not a choice.

# APPENDIX A
## SURVEY INSTRUMENT—WITHOUT RESPONSES

**WIFS** SURVEY OF HIGHLY SUCCESSFUL WOMEN IN FINANCIAL SERVICES

The goal of this survey is to examine the career and life paths of highly successful female financial "advisors" across the financial services industry. The survey represents a beginning step to determine how better to attract, develop, and advance the careers of women in our industry. The results of the survey are expected to be published by GAMA.

All of the information you provide is confidential. Your individual data and responses will not be cited in the article and your name will not be used in this or any future publication without your permission.

---

1. My gender is:

2. Current Age:

3. Marital Status:

4. Number and Current Ages of Children:

5. Within which range does your annual gross income from insurance and investment products fall?

6. I first entered the financial services industry at age:

7. My highest level of education is:

8. My first job in the industry was:

9. When I started in the business I worked with:

10. I entered the financial services industry for the following reason:

11. I have stayed in the business because of:

12. After I started in the financial services industry, I left and re-entered it:

13. Do you feel it is more difficult for women to succeed in the financial services industry?

14. The word that best describes my career path in the financial services industry is:

15. My current job in the industry is:

16. I have built my clientele primarily through:

17. I attribute my success in the financial services industry to:

18. I currently have the following professional designations (check all that apply and specify "other"):

19. I belong to the following professional organizations:

20. The assets I have under management are:

21. I qualified for MDRT or other company/industry honors (please specify honor in Comment Section below) in my _____ year in business:

22. The biggest challenge to my success has been?

23. _____ motivates me to succeed:

24. How long did it take you to achieve a 6-figure income?

25. I hired my first staff member in my _____ year in business:

26. I currently employ _____ people:

27. I currently work:

28. My current work environment is:

29. I have stayed in the business because of:

30. My clients are primarily (if other, please specify below):

31. My primary line of business is:

32. Below please provide additional information about how you have been SUCCESSFUL in the financial services industry.

33. Below please complete the following sentence: I believe that more women would be successful in the financial services industry if_____.

34. I am willing to be interviewed by a WIFS board member for future articles/book.

35. This survey has been designed to be anonymous. If you would like to receive survey result information, please provide your e-mail address.

Reprinted with permission by WIFS board of directors

# WOMEN IN FINANCIAL SERVICES: HOW TO SUCCEED IN BUSINESS

Reprinted with permission from the November/December 2012 issue of the *GAMA International Journal*. Copyright © 2012 GAMA International

# HOW TO SUCCEED IN BUSINESS

> Women have become the new game changers in our industry, point out **ARTHEA "CHARLIE" REED, PH.D., CLTC** and **KAREN ROBERTS, CLU CHFC**. To gain a better understanding of how women operate, what really motivates their business decisions, and how they think, first look at the numbers.

WE ALL APPRECIATE the growing importance of women to the insurance and financial services industry, not only as clients but also as agents and managers. So this past spring, Women in Insurance and Financial Services (WIFS) conducted an extensive survey called the *WIFS Survey of Women in the Financial Services Industry*, which involved female agents, managers, brokers, and financial planners. The goal was to try to retrace the career paths of the most financially successful women in the industry and determine how taking those routes helped bring them such achievement.

The data from the survey, along with both anecdotal evidence from respondents' surveys and in-depth interviews with select respondents, should help WIFS and other organizations in the financial services industry better recruit, train, and retain women and turn them into high-powered agents and managers. Along with educating financial services leaders on this important strategy to secure the future of our industry, the aim is to help female representation and success in the financial services industry reach the levels of other professions, such as law, medicine, and accounting.

The survey turned up a great deal of important information and feedback. Following are some of the highlights.

## Support for Women in Financial Services

One recurring theme that arose in the anonymous comments of survey respondents was that although the financial services industry is still perceived as male dominated, its impact on the success of women ranges from none at all to presenting a challenge to causing downright frustration and anger. One respondent summarized the situation with, "Companies need to better learn how to leverage the talents and abilities that women inherently have [networking, relationships, compassion], and only when this happens will women feel like they truly have a place in what has traditionally been a male-dominated profession."

### MENTORS

At the same time, many respondents said their male mentors, including their fathers and husbands (9 percent of all respondents reported starting in the industry by working with family), were extremely important to their growth and eventual success.

Whether male or female, a women advisor's mentor is viewed as vital to the advisor's success. In addition, women responded that seeing successful female role models makes it easier for them to believe in their own success. "My company's president is a woman, five out of seven senior planners are women, and four out of six junior planners are women," wrote another respondent

## BEHIND THE WIFS SURVEY

For the *WIFS Survey of Women in the Financial Services Industry*, a total of 794 forms were completed by female field professionals who spanned the financial services profession — from insurance agents or representatives to wealth managers to fee-based financial planners. Respondents included self-employed businesses owners; employees or representatives of major insurance companies, banks, wire houses, and trust companies; and independent brokers who provide employee and executive benefits or help families with investments and financial planning.

The survey forms were distributed to all WIFS members. In addition, WIFS corporate partners, including Guardian Life Insurance Company of America, Lincoln Financial Group, MassMutual Financial Group, MetLife, New York Life Insurance Company, Northwestern Mutual Life Insurance Company, The Penn Mutual Life Insurance Company, The Prudential Insurance Company of America, Thrivent Financial for Lutherans, and Transamerica Agency Network — distributed forms either to their entire female field force or to a select group of top female producers. The survey was also available on wifsnational.org and on WIFS's LinkedIn and Facebook pages. Plus, WIFS invited certain female leaders of other professional organizations to take part.

in the survey feedback. "I feel that women are very successful in the financial planning business."

### TEAMS

Teamwork also plays a large role in the success of women, and that's particularly evident in the early years of a career. Fifty percent of the highest-compensated women work with either a partner or on a team. Successful teams pick and choose people to work with various clients, depending on each advisor's personality and strengths as well as the client's personality and needs.

### FAMILY

Another key to women's success is the support of a spouse and family, said respondents. Many described the struggle to find a balance between caring for children and working in a career that demands so much of their time, particularly in the first few years. A number of women who consider themselves successful wrote about how they could not have succeeded in the career without having a supportive spouse, often one who provides much of the child care.

# FOLLOWING THE NUMBERS

Women included in the *WIFS Survey of Women in the Financial Services Industry* represent all income levels. About 43 percent earn less than $75,000; 25 percent earn from $75,000 to $124,999; 17 percent, $125,000 to $199,999; 13 percent, $200,000 to $499,999; 2 percent, $500,000 to $999,999; and 1 percent, $1 million or more. Following are some ways that female financial services professionals with annual incomes greater than $500,000 compare with their less successful counterparts, according to the WIFS survey.

## Getting Started

- One hundred percent of women earning $1 million–plus in annual gross and 47 percent of women earning $500,000 to $999,999 start in the business between the ages of 20 and 25; instead, only 23 percent of women with incomes under $75,000 join the business from ages 20 to 25.
- A substantial minority of all women (15 to 25 percent) begin as office staff.
- Nearly 63 percent of women with annual incomes of $1 million or higher hold bachelor's degrees; 25 percent of these have advanced degrees.
- Nearly 53 percent of women earning $500,000 to $999,999 have at least a bachelor's degree; 24 percent of these have advanced degrees.
- Forty-four percent of women earning less than $75,000 have bachelor's degrees; 20 percent of these have advanced degrees.

## Earnings

- More than 50 percent of respondents who earn $200,000 to $1 million or more said they qualified for MDRT or other company or industry honors within the first five years in the business, versus 30 percent of women who bring in $75,000 to $124,999, and just 9 percent of women who earn less than $75,000.

## Clientele

- The most financially successful women build their clientele primarily through referrals, including 50 percent of women earning $1 million or more and 41 percent of women earning $500,000 to $999,999. Of women making less than $75,000, 27 percent acquire referrals through networking. A minority of all groups (8 to 18 percent) reported building a clientele through "high activity," which includes making phone calls to schedule appointments and conducting face-to-face meetings. Typically, at least 20 phone contacts are needed to set five appointments, with four kept appointments per day.
- The higher the income level, the more likely that the woman's clients are primarily professionals:

About 50 percent of women with incomes of $1 million or more work primarily with professionals, and 25 percent work mainly with small-business owners, respondents reported. Only 9 percent of women earning less than $75,000 work chiefly with professionals, while 30 percent work mainly with families.

- Women with primarily female clients tend to earn less. Twelve percent of women respondents earning less than $75,000 said that their clients were mainly women. None of the respondents who reported earning more than $1 million indicated this to be true.

## Staff

- The most financially successful women hire staff early in their careers. In fact, 63 percent of the most successful respondents hired staff within one to three years, and 50 percent of those did so in their first year. Of the least financially successful group, only 11 percent said they hired staff within the first three years. In addition, 74 percent of women earning less than $75,000 said they currently have no employees, while 50 percent of the most financially successful women have five to 15 staff members.

## Designations

- Seventy-five percent of women earning more than $1 million per year and 80 percent of those earning $500,000 to $999,999 have one or more professional designations (such as CLU, ChFC, or CFP). A third of women earning less than $75,000 and 59 percent of women making $75,000 to $124,999 have at least one professional designation.

## Motivations

- Nearly 38 percent of the most successful respondents entered the business for the income, whereas only 15 percent of the lowest-earning respondents were focused on income. The percentage of women entering the business for income increases with each income level.

# FOLLOWING THE NUMBERS

### Marital Status

- A larger percentage of women at the highest income levels are married, including 87 percent with incomes of $1,000,000-plus and 82 percent with incomes over $500,000. More than 56 percent of women with incomes under $75,000 and 61 percent of women earning $75,000 to $124,999 are married.

### Industry Challenges

- The most financially successful are more likely to attribute their business success (63 percent), as well as challenges (50 percent), to themselves. Likewise, 63 percent of women earning more than $1,000,000 are more likely to answer no to the question "Do you feel it is more difficult for women to succeed in the financial services industry?" Among the least financially successful group of women, 27 percent attribute their success to themselves, and more than 35 percent call themselves their biggest challenge. And 51 percent of women earning less than $75,000 believe that women have a more difficult time in the financial services industry.

## COMPANY

A significant minority of respondents mentioned the importance of their supervisor's and company's willingness to help females achieve a satisfactory work-life balance. One woman reported that she had been successful in the financial services industry because her company's training and work hours for new hires were geared toward balancing work-life needs. Unfortunately, most respondents reported having had the opposite experience: They had to adapt to their new role in a less flexible and less supportive environment.

## SELF

At the same time, a sizable portion of survey respondents wrote that more women would be successful in the financial services industry if they believed in themselves and had more self-confidence. Many noted that they are successful because they are confident, take responsibility for achieving their goals, always put the needs of the client first, are reliable and great with follow-up, and are simply good at what they do.

## Perseverance Pays Off

"Keeping the client first" was a mantra echoed by most respondents, and this includes remaining persistent and always trying to do the right thing for the client. The best ways to really get to know the client's wants and needs are by keeping in touch with clients throughout their careers and into retirement, and by asking a lot of questions, listening, and taking notes. Following up with in-person discussion is essential to building the relationship.

Many survey respondents talked about the need for the industry to move from a male-centric culture to one that is more supportive of the talents and needs of women. "It's a matter of creating a culture which includes everything from the visual representation, to the language that is used, to recognition in front of peers and others," said one respondent. "The more women are included in these areas, the more women not in the profession may think, 'Maybe I can do that.'"

If woman are to succeed in our industry, we as managers must nurture them at the onset of their careers. Just as in life, the early years can lay the foundation for career-long success. ♠

LEARN MORE    LOG ON to GAMASOURCE    Visit These Learning Tracks

» **Arthea "Charlie" Reed, Ph.D., CLTC,** has been a financial representative with Northwestern Mutual Life Insurance Company and owner of Long Term Care Insurance Connection since 1996. She focuses her practice on retirement planning and long-term-care insurance for executives, businesses, and professional practices. She is on the WIFS board of directors. Before entering her career in financial services she was a university professor and administrator and the author or coauthor of 14 books in the fields of education and adolescent literature. She is the principal author of the *WIFS Survey of Women in the Financial Services Industry.* Charlie can be reached at charlie.reed@nmfn.com.

» **Karen Roberts, CLU ChFC,** is a wealth planning specialist with more than 21 years of experience. Karen currently serves as the national president of Women in Insurance and Financial Services (WIFS). She is past president of the WIFS Gold Coast chapter and was previously president of the Broward County chapter of the American Society of Financial Services Professionals. Karen can be reached at karan.roberts@lfg.com.

240

# APPENDIX C
# INITIAL INTERVIEW QUESTIONS FOR
# WOMEN SELECTED TO APPEAR IN BOOK

## QUESTIONS FOR YOUR WRITTEN COMMENTS

Feel free to respond to these questions on this e-mail, a separate e-mail, or attach a Word document. We will notify you when we receive your responses.

1. Describe your current "business model." Consider including some or all of the following (or simply go your own way):

   - If you have done a one-page business plan or some other planning instrument or you have a marketing piece or website that describes your business and are willing to share it/them with Diane and Charlie, please attach it or provide us with a link to it.
   - Business name, if other than the corporation with whom you are affiliated.
   - Your designations/degrees
   - Your typical A-plus client (i.e., couple with more than $3 million in liquid assets or closely held business with more than 10 employees)

- Type of work you do for your A-plus client (i.e., financial planning, insurance, and investments for individuals and couples; voluntary group benefits, executive benefits for closely-held businesses, or BOLI/COLI)
- Do you work alone, with partner(s), or as a part of a team?
- How many employees do you have? How many employees does your business or team have? What are their roles?
- Describe your typical business day.

2. Remembering back to your early days in the financial services industry, what things/people/events/organizations/relationships/educational opportunities were important to your professional development? Consider including some of the following (if appropriate):

- List any of the following: boss/manager/mentor/coach/friend/family member/teacher/other who truly made a positive difference in your professional growth. Feel free to tell a story if you would like.
- An event/incident/moment that was incredibly important to your career. (May not have been positive when it occurred but had an incredibly positive outcome in terms of your professional growth.)
- The best elements of your "training."
- "I couldn't have succeeded in this business without _____."

3. Switching gears: Were there any things that occurred in your early years in the business that could have caused you to quit or made it more difficult for you to succeed?

4. How did the people/events of your personal life affect your professional growth?

- How did you juggle your personal life/relationships/responsibilities with a very demanding profession?
- What advice would you give a daughter or niece if she were entering the business?

5. Are there things/events/people/training and education/decisions that could have made you even more successful than you are?

6. What goals do you have for your business in the next five to ten years? How do you plan to transition your business in the next five to ten years? Consider including, if appropriate:

   - Your succession plan.
   - What you need help with if you are to achieve your goals. Who could provide that help?

7. How have you balanced your personal life with your business life?

8. Have you had any leadership roles in your company or the industry? If yes, please describe and discuss how these have affected your business.

9. What else would you like us to know and be willing to share about you, your business, or your family?

# APPENDIX D
## PROFESSIONAL DESIGNATIONS AND ORGANIZATIONS: ACRONYMS, DESCRIPTIONS, AND WEBSITES

## TABLE 1: PROFESSIONAL DESIGNATIONS

| ACRONYM | DESCRIPTION OF PROFESSIONAL DESIGNATION |
| --- | --- |
| AAMS | Accredited Asset Management Specialist |
| ADPA | Accredited Domestic Partnership Advisor |
| APMA | Accredited Portfolio Management Advisor |
| AWMA | Accredited Wealth Management Advisor |
| CAP® | Chartered Advisor in Philanthropy |
| CASL | Chartered Advisor for Senior Living |
| CFA | Chartered Financial Analyst |
| CFDP | Certified Financial Divorce Practitioner |
| CFP® | Certified Financial Planner |
| ChHC | Chartered Healthcare Consultant |
| CHRS | Certified Human Resources Specialist |
| ChSNC | Chartered Special Needs Consultant |
| CLF | Chartered Leadership Fellow |
| CLTC | Certified Long-Term Care |
| CLU | Chartered Life Underwriter |
| CMFC | Chartered Mutual Fund Counselor |
| CPA | Certified Public Accountant |

| | |
|---|---|
| CRPC® | Chartered Retirement Planning Counselor |
| CRPS | Chartered Retirement Plans Specialist |
| CSA | Certified Senior Advisor |
| FIC | Fraternal Insurance Counselor |
| FLMI | Fellow Life Management Institute |
| FSCP | Financial Services Certified Professional |
| LUTCF | Life Underwriter Training Council Fellow |
| MSFS | Master of Science in Financial Services |
| MSM | Master of Science in Management |
| PhD | PhD in Financial and Retirement Planning |
| REBC | Registered Employee Benefits Consultant |
| RFC | Registered Financial Consultant |
| RICP | Retirement Income Certified Professional |
| RP | Registered Paraplanner |

| WEBSITE | DESCRIPTION OF SPONSORING ORGANIZATIONS |
|---|---|
| www.theamericancollege.edu | The American College of Financial Services |
| www.cffpinfo.com | College for Financial Planning® |
| www.cfp.net | CFP Board of Standards, Inc. |
| www.loma.org | Life Office Management Association |
| www.naifa.org | National Association of Insurance and Financial Advisors |

## TABLE 2: PROFESSIONAL ORGANIZATIONS

| ACRONYM | DESCRIPTION OF PROFESSIONAL ASSOCIATIONS | WEBSITE |
|---|---|---|
| AALU | Association of Advanced Life Underwriters | www.aalu.org |
| AHIA | Association of Health Insurance Advisors | www.ahia.net |
| FPA | Financial Planning Association | www.plannersearch.org |
| FSP | Society of Financial Service Professionals | www.financialpro.org |
| GAMA | General Agents Management Association | www.gamaweb.com |
| MDRT | Million Dollar Round Table | www.mdrt.org |
| NAHU | National Association of Health Underwriters | www.nahu.org |
| NAIFA | National Association of Insurance and Financial Advisors | www.naifa.org |
| WIFS | Women in Insurance and Financial Services | www.wifsnational.org |

# BIBLIOGRAPHY

Baldrige, Letitia. *Juggling: The Art of Balancing Marriage, Motherhood, and a Career.* New York: Viking, 1976.

Certified Financial Planner (CFP) Board of Standards. *Making More Room for Women in the Financial Planning Profession* (April 2014).

*ForbesBrandVoice*™, *Northwestern MutualVoice.* Video interview of Delynn Dolan Alexander, 2014.

Granum, O. Alfred, Barry Alberstein, and Delia Alberstein. *Building a Financial Services Clientele: The Ultimate Guide to the One Card System.* Erlanger, KY: The National Underwriter Company, 2014. Originally published in 1968.

Hyde, Catherine Ryan. *Pay It Forward.* New York: Simon and Schuster, 2000.

Hyde, Catherine Ryan. *The Pay it Forward Foundation.* San Luis Obispo, California.

Keuneke, Kathryn Furlaw. "A Balanced Approach: Borislow's strength as a leader comes from a commitment to balance family and business," *Round the Table: Official Publication of the Million Dollar Round Table* (September/October 2011): 44-47.

Leder, Mimi. *Pay It Forward*. Los Angeles: Warner Brothers Pictures, 2000.

Lipman, Joanne. "Women at Work: A Guide for Men," *Wall Street Journal*, December 13–14, C1.

Miller, Claire Cain. "Even among Harvard Graduates, Women Fall Short of their Work Expectations." The Upshot. Edited by David Leonhardt. *New York Times*, November 28, 2014. http://www.ny-times.com/upshot.

Nightingale, Earl. *The Strangest Secret*. La Vergne, TN: BN Publishing, 2011. Originally a spoken-word recording, 1956. Corey Dahl, "A Career Change Gone Right," *Life Insurance Selling*, May 2013, 12–16.

O'Donnell, Colleen, and Lynn Baker. *Generous Kids: Helping Your Child Experience the Joy of Giving*. Dallas: Brown Books Publishing, 2007.

Reed, Arthea, and Karen Roberts. "Women in Financial Services: How to Succeed in Business," *GAMA International Journal* (November/December 2012): 42–46.

Sandberg, Sheryl. *Lean In: Women, Work, and the Will to Lead*. New York: Knopf, 2013.

"Where Are the Women? A new IRI Study Sheds Light on Why So Few Women Choose to Become Financial Advisors." *Financial Planning*, June 2013, B6–B7.

WIFS board of directors, *WIFS Survey for Highly Successful Women in the Financial Services Industry* (2012), unpublished.

Yost, Cali William. *Tweak It: Make What Matters Happen to You Every Day*. New York: Center Street Publishing, 2013.

# ABOUT THE AUTHORS

**ARTHEA (CHARLIE) REED, PHD, CLTC**, is currently a senior financial representative with Northwestern Mutual and senior partner of Long-Term Care Insurance Connection.

Prior to joining the financial services industry as a director of recruiting and training in her husband Donald's Asheville, North Carolina, district agency in 1996, she was a professor and chair of the Education Department at the University of North Carolina–Asheville (UNCA). She joined the faculty of the university in 1978 after com-

Charlie Reed with her husband, Don, in the wine country of South Africa

pleting her PhD at Florida State University. During her eighteen-year tenure at UNCA, she authored or coauthored fourteen books, edited an international journal in the field of adolescent literature, authored and edited teaching guides of classic literature for Viking/Penguin, and was the Feldman Professor of Research and Service. Today she is a UNCA professor emeritus.

In 1998, Charlie recruited herself and became a financial representative and long-term care specialist with Northwestern Mutual. She also founded Long-Term Care Insurance Connection, a company working with businesses and organizations in placing and administering long-term care insurance plans for their executives, employees, and members. She has spoken widely in the United States and Canada on the topic of long term-care planning.

From 1998 until 2011, she led Northwestern Mutual eleven times in long-term care insurance sales. In 2012, she transitioned Long-Term Care Insurance Connection to her successor Barbara DeBerry, now managing partner and owner of the business. She also qualified for Million Dollar Round Table (MDRT), Court of the Table, and Top of the Table every year since 1979. She served two years on the board of Women in Insurance and Financial Services (WIFS) and authored The *WIFS Survey for Highly Successfully Women in the Financial Services Industry* completed in 2012. This is her first book in the field of financial services.

Today, Charlie and her husband divide their time between Asheville and Hilton Head, South Carolina.

**DIANE DIXON, CLU**, coach, and owner of 3FCoaching (Faith Focus Follow Through), a national coaching business providing dynamic business and life planning and nutritious support and accountability to the ambitious and determined who want to live a larger life on purpose.

Diane Dixon at the Chapel of the Holy Cross in Sedona, Arizona.

Diane is a national past president of Women in Insurance and Financial Services (WIFS). She is a graduate of Coach University, a member of International Coach Federation (ICF), a consultant of the One Page Business Plan™, and a practitioner with Leading From Your Strengths™.

Diane coaches many financial advisors and their teams; 2015 marks Diane's thirty-eighth year in the financial services industry. Prior to launching her full-time coaching practice, Diane was a financial representative with Northwestern Mutual in Louisville, Kentucky. She qualified for numerous company and industry awards. She moved to Milwaukee, Wisconsin, in 1996 to join the corporate team of Northwestern Mutual before returning to Ohio in 2000 to launch her coaching practice.

In 2007, Diane coauthored *Magnificent Masters in Financial Services*, and in 2008, she was named Woman of the Year by Women in Insurance and Financial Services (WIFS). Diane resides in Xenia, Ohio.

# ENDNOTES

1   WIFS board of directors, *WIFS Survey for Highly Successful Women in the Financial Services Industry* (2012), unpublished.

2   Certified financial Planner (CFP) Board of Standards, *Making More Room for Women in the Financial Planning Profession* (April 2014).

3   Women in Insurance and Financial Services (WIFS), http://www.wifsnational.org.

4   Million Dollar Round Table (MDRT), http://www.mdrt.org.

5   Arthea Reed and Karen Roberts, "Women in Financial Services: How to Succeed in Business," *GAMA International Journal* (November/December 2012): 42–46.

6   WIFS board of directors.

7   Reed and Roberts.

8   O. Alfred Granum, Barry Alberstein, and Delia Alberstein, *Building a Financial Services Clientele: The Ultimate Guide to the One Card System* (Erlanger, KY: The National Underwriter Company, 2014), originally published in 1968.

9   WIFS board of directors.

10  Earl Nightingale, *The Strangest Secret* (La Vergne, TN: BN Publishing, 2011), originally a spoken-word recording, 1956.

11  Corey Dahl, "A Career Change Gone Right," *Life Insurance Selling*, May 2013, 12–16.

12  CFP Board of Standards, 3.

13  "Where Are the Women? A new IRI Study Sheds Light on Why So Few Women Choose to Become Financial Advisors," *Financial Planning*, June 2013, B6–B7.

14  CFP Board of Standards, 3.

15  CFP Board of Standards, 4.

16  CFP Board of Standards, 7-8.

17  CFP Board of Standards, 11.

18  CFP Board of Standards, 11.

19  CFP Board of Standards, 11.

20  CFP Board of Standards, 23.

21  CFP Board of Standards, 23.

22  CFP Board of Standards, 24.

23  CFP Board of Standards, 24.

24  Letitia Baldridge, *Juggling: The Art of Balancing Marriage, Motherhood, and a Career* (New York: Viking, 1976).

25  *ForbesBrandVoice™, Northwestern MutualVoice*, video interview of Delynn Dolan Alexander, 2014.

26  Cali William Yost, *Tweak It: Make What Matters Happen to You Every Day* (New York: Center Street Publishing, 2013).

27  WIFS board of directors.

28  CFP Board of Standards, 27.

29  CFP Board of Standards, 28.

30  CFP Board of Standards, 11.

31  Joanne Lipman, "Women at Work: A Guide for Men," *Wall Street Journal*, December 13–14, C1.

32  Sheryl Sandberg, *Lean In: Women, Work, and the Will to Lead* (New York: Knopf, 2013), 62.

33  Mimi Leder, director, *Pay It Forward* (Los Angeles: Warner Brothers Pictures, 2000).

34  Catherine Ryan Hyde, *Pay It Forward* (New York: Simon and Schuster, 2000).

35  Catherine Ryan Hyde, founder, *The Pay it Forward Foundation*, San Luis Obispo, CA.

36  Colleen O'Donnell and Lynn Baker, *Generous Kids: Helping Your Child Experience the Joy of Giving* (Dallas: Brown Books Publishing, 2007).

37  Claire Cain Miller, "Even among Harvard Graduates, Women Fall Short of their Work Expectations," In The Upshot, edited by David Leonhardt, *New York Times*, November 28, 2014, http://www.nytimes.com/upshot.

38  CFP Board of Standards, 23-24.

39  CFP Board of Standards, 20-23

## Open Book Editions
## A Berrett-Koehler Partner

Open Book Editions is a joint venture between Berrett-Koehler Publishers and Author Solutions, the market leader in self-publishing. There are many more aspiring authors who share Berrett-Koehler's mission than we can sustainably publish. To serve these authors, Open Book Editions offers a comprehensive self-publishing opportunity.

### A Shared Mission

Open Book Editions welcomes authors who share the Berrett-Koehler mission—Creating a World That Works for All. We believe that to truly create a better world, action is needed at all levels—individual, organizational, and societal. At the individual level, our publications help people align their lives with their values and with their aspirations for a better world. At the organizational level, we promote progressive leadership and management practices, socially responsible approaches to business, and humane and effective organizations. At the societal level, we publish content that advances social and economic justice, shared prosperity, sustainability, and new solutions to national and global issues.

Open Book Editions represents a new way to further the BK mission and expand our community. We look forward to helping more authors challenge conventional thinking, introduce new ideas, and foster positive change.

For more information, see the Open Book Editions website:
http://www.iuniverse.com/Packages/OpenBookEditions.aspx

Join the BK Community! See exclusive author videos, join discussion groups, find out about upcoming events, read author blogs, and much more! http://bkcommunity.com/

CPSIA information can be obtained
at www.ICGtesting.com
Printed in the USA
FFOW04n1913210815
16184FF